In Praise of
*The Inspiring Journeys of Pi_*

Jane has interviewed very special women who are in touch with their passion and hearts. She has a gift of bringing each one alive through her empathy and personal connection with each one. An inspiring book which I am sure will encourage many to take risks and follow their hearts.

JO BERRY
Peace Ambassador, Building Bridges for Peace Co-founder, with Patrick Magee,
the man who murdered her father, Sir Anthony Berry (MP), in the IRA Brighton Bombing.
www.buildingbridgesforpeace.org

Once again Jane presents a collection of personal stories which are inspiring and fascinating: and all the more so because they are true. These stories are very different from each other but also essentially the same: every woman has to fight to achieve her aims. These are the stories of exceptional women, but in a sense aren't we all exceptional, and shouldn't we all celebrate the Pilgrim Mother we carry within ourselves?

LORELY BURT, MP
Liberal Democrat MP for Solihull, first female Chair of the
Liberal Democrat Parliamentary Party
www.lorelyburt.org.uk/en/

Jane is an inspirational lady who shows us the way to follow our hearts to become true Pilgrim Mothers. Her wonderful crusade to harness the feminine way of living our lives and doing business is truly revolutionary. Jane's stories of women who change the world with the power of their courage and hard work give us the faith to believe our dreams will also come true.

DEBORAH HADFIELD
Award-winning Film Director
www.queenbeefilms.com

Jane, the Pilgrim Mother, is a modern spiritual scribe sharing women's stories interspersed with her own, inspiring a generation of women to celebrate themselves, their successes and their transformative power. These stories make us aware of our inner-Pilgrim and why it is vital to be proud of our achievements as female leaders. Jane's writing makes us stop and look at where in our lives we have served and made a difference and to not dismiss those acts as having no value. The stories of our lives are the recipes we can hand down to inspire the next generation of spiritual female leaders. Jane is showing us how this can be done with such clarity and grace. This is how you create a hopeful future.

MOIRA BUSH
Founder of Silver Spheres healing system and the Spiritual Entrepreneurs Academy
UK Representative of Colour Mirrors
www.moirabush.com

This book is just fabulous! Jane is very gentle in the way she extracts these stories and that's her gift — to give these outstanding women this platform to share their stories. She really captures how courageous most women of achievement are. The book is truly inspiring. These women's journeys highlight brilliantly how brave women are in finding their calling and achieving what they are capable of.

VIV J PARRY
Owner and Founder of Exquisite Handmade Cakes Ltd
www.exquisitehandmadecakes.co.uk

It's both an honour and a privilege to have the opportunity to sing Jane Noble Knight's praises in this inspirational book. Jane is noble by name and by nature. She has a unique talent that allows her to get right to the heart of each of the individual women pioneers she has interviewed for this book. Her heartfelt empathy and humility shines through in each unique story and keeps you captivated and enthralled throughout. There is real authenticity and truth without ego in these transmissions. Within that vulnerability and fragility is a beauty and rawness that we can all relate to.

This book is timely. The inspiring stories of these wonderful women's journeys serve to hold our own hands and encourage us forward on our own unique paths. The time has truly arrived for us all to shine. We too can find the courage to move forward with our own ideas and creativity. Each story and experience clears the runway and makes it easier for others to follow.

As I read each individual tale, I find I am transported to a brave and heroic new world, a world that supports, encourages, collaborates, builds community, and is kind and loving. This new world is a land of plenty, where there is room for everyone.

Within these stories Jane has captured a magical blend of creativity and a hope for humanity as a whole. They have the capacity to reconnect you to the world of love and miracle, and to follow your dreams, your bliss, and to never, ever give up.

SURYAH MAGDA RAY
Co-founder, LoveDansing
www.lovedansing.com

This book is a goldmine of inspiration!

The second book in this best-selling *The Inspiring Journeys* series blew me away. The stories are as individual and inspiring as those of the entrepreneurs in *The Inspiring Journeys of Women Entrepreneurs*, but this book's interviewees are, naturally, totally different.

There are personal stories as diverse as Sue Allan's spellbinding account of her modern-day connection with a woman who helped the original Pilgrim Mothers in their escape to the New World; international best-selling author Katherine Woodward Thomas's insights; Soup Sister Partner, Suki Kaur-Cosier; award-winning stand-up comedian Shelley Bridgman, and many more gems that all epitomise the spirit summed up in Diane Ackerman's quote:

'I don't want to get to the end of my life and find that I just lived the length of it. I want to have lived the width of it as well.'

I've come away from this book with Jane Noble Knight's question ringing in my ears: *'Are you pioneering your way to your most authentic life?'*

Anne Risaria Langley
Scriptwriter, Director of Not Only Angels Ltd
www.notonlyangels.co.uk

In Praise of
The Inspiring Journeys of Women Entrepreneurs and Jane Noble Knight

If we are the Pilgrim Mothers then Jane Noble Knight is the 'Mothership' in which we sail to a brave new world of loving-kindness, oneness, faith, hope and integrity – values which the Feminine has always represented throughout time.

RACHEL ELNAUGH
Founder of Red Letter Days, star of BBC TV's Dragons' Den series 1 and 2
www.rachelelnaugh.com

At this time of personal and planetary transformation, women like Jane Noble Knight are unearthing stories, myths and women leading legendary lives to inspire and encourage us all on our pilgrimage to our own Truth. By reading this book you will voyage on a journey and find yourself inspired, uplifted and encouraged to make your life your greatest adventure!

KATHARINE DEVER
Intuitive Business Coach
www.katharinedever.com

Jane Noble Knight is a special knight with a noble cause. Every knight in history fought for revolutionary change. In this inaugural book, Jane presents a blueprint for global change. Her personal journey is a call for each one of us to embark on our own transformation. This book provides the guiding light along the journey for each one of us to embrace a new pathway for human evolution. The time is now. The way is clear. The wisdom contained here is eminently practical. All it needs is for you to say: Here I am – use me. Women hold the answer to bring about this much needed change! Their united power is waiting to be gathered and unleashed. Heed the call or ignore this book at your peril!

DR. DAVID PAUL
Specialist in Large-Scale, Complex Change & Eupsyhian Leadership
Best-selling Author of *Life and Work: Challenging Economic Man*
dpaul@attwise.com

It is our time…

I have felt for many years that our time was coming, and now it is here. And so Jane has 'timed' the publication of this book to perfection. It is time for us women to step into our power, which we know is within each of us. It is time for us to believe in ourselves again and help move the world to a better place. It is time not only for us to dream, but to live our dreams.

The female pioneers blazing the trail, some of whom Jane has written about in this book, have shown us that we can all do this. But it is up to us to believe in ourselves when others don't and to know that there is a better way when others say there isn't. We all can turn our dreams into reality and be the amazing woman we were born to be. And our time is now!

SUSAN HARPER TODD

Only British woman to sail the Atlantic *and* climb Everest. First British female leader of an Everest expedition and only the fifth British woman to have reached the summit of Everest.
www.susanharpertodd.com

Jane Noble Knight's books offer the opportunity to study and immerse oneself in the lives of other women: extraordinary women who somehow still manage to be every woman. We are all on a quest. Some of us have grown weary, some have been misled. Some have strayed from the path of freedom, creativity and love. And some of us are looking for angelic messenger voices that will guide us into the light. Jane's books offer a gathering of loving, inspirational, gentle yet strong she-voices. You can read and relax, and let the truth of the testimonies of these women sink in, like an enriching moisturiser into dry skin.

JAN TCHAMANI

Prize-winning Author, Communications Director of The Red Tent (Heart of England)
burjan@blueyonder.co.uk

Once I read 'one of the secrets of success was the unconditional support of your opposite sex parent'. For me it's been just so true. The love and 'alwaysthereness' of my mother was the underlying force in all my early success. As time goes by, more and more mother figures appear in one's life, each with an appropriate and invariably timely lesson to be shared.

What better, then, for men (and I suppose for women too!) than a collection of female wisdom, inspiration and a dose of pioneering spirit to lift our hearts and set us again to the path.

Jane Noble Knight is described so aptly by her name. Working closely with her for over a year showed me her true character, her outward-focused-ness and her love of her fellow traveller on this spinning blue.

Read on, smile, think and act on the lessons she's extracted so carefully for our use – will you?

PETER THOMSON

'The UK's Most Prolific Information Product Creator'
www.peterthomson.com

Rarely in life do you meet someone who really walks the talk and embodies their message and life's work. Jane Noble Knight is one such inspirational woman. Selfless in her devotion to empowering others, she positively breathes her passion and absolutely is 'The Pilgrim Mother'. Read Jane's stories and prepare to be changed.

SHELLEY BRIDGMAN

Keynote Speaker, Psychotherapist, Stand-Up Comic
TV and Radio Commentator, Author of *Stand-Up For Your Self*
www.stand-upforyourself.com

I think what you're creating is so beautiful. You're an inspiration to women. I read a couple of years back, and it was a great validation to my instincts, that people really need role models in order to move forward in life. Concepts or insights alone are not enough. What people really need, in order to embody change, are role models – people who have done it. That is what you're doing – providing role models.

KATHERINE WOODWARD THOMAS
Best-selling Author of *Calling In "The One"*, Co-Creator of *Feminine Power*
www.katherinewoodwardthomas.com

Jane Noble Knight has done what many women only dream about. She's followed her passion and let her heart lead her to her truth, and in turn empowering women, just like you, to freely unleash the quietened mother, healer, nurturer and lover, and discover a life filled with possibility and passion.

Eliciting stories that move the reader to explore her uniqueness is what Jane does best. Simply inspiring – can't wait to read the next book.

VANESSA MCLEAN
Co-Author of *Fight For Your Dreams: The Power of Never Giving up*
www.vanessamclean.com

When I first met Jane, I was taken by her gentleness and warmth, together with her desire to understand more about herself and the role of women in business and the wider world. And when she spoke about her 'pilgrimage', it was clear that she was going to create something unique and special – which she has. The world needs to wake up to the power of authenticity, of living our own truths and being brave enough to step out of the mainstream views when they don't fit with our own life purpose. This is precisely what Jane has done and her mission and book is inspiring to both women AND men, who equally need to hear her message.

PAUL HARRIS
Writer, Speaker, Coach and Founder of The Real Academy
www.real-success.co.uk

It's still tough for us ladies in the business arena, but Jane's informative and inspirational take on it really motivates and guides you! Having had the pleasure of filming with Jane a few years ago, I knew instantly that this very calming, kind but dynamic lady had something a little bit special about her. We all knew she would go on to do something a tad out of the ordinary but interesting. Hence, I wanted to stay in contact and see where her journey took her! This book is a fabulous vehicle for her, and exploring the greatness of her fellow females is completely apt. Jane herself is such a generous-spirited lady with an abundance of knowledge and warmth that she radiates. It's no surprise that this is her path...... What next, Jane? .... Bravo Jane, we love what you're doing!

SUNITA SHROFF
Presenter, Actress, Property Expert and Red Carpet Reporter
www.sunitashroff.com

Tucked up in bed, one night, I thought I would just read a few pages ... Within seconds I was gripped and couldn't put the book down.

I've read several personal growth books. This particular one is written so beautifully and authentically, I really wanted to keep reading to find out more about the author's journey and what we could learn from these inspirational and pioneering women.

Jane has hand-picked some very wise women from our industry whose insights and honesty are both profound and refreshing. They installed a feeling of excitement and possibility within me as I read on.

Jane has a gift of pulling all this wisdom together in a way that makes you feel that it's not only possible for these women but possible for women everywhere!

With this compilation Jane has brought a much-needed gift to the world.

Thank you.

LUCIE BRADBURY
CEO of Damsels in Success - the Transformational Network for Female Entrepreneurs
www.damselsinsuccess.co.uk

THE INSPIRING JOURNEYS OF PILGRIM MOTHERS

To Sandra,

fabulous Pilgrim Mother.

I'm so pleased we have

connected on our inspiring journeys.

Many happy journeys ahead!

Love Jane / xx   20/8/13

THE
INSPIRING
JOURNEYS
OF PILGRIM MOTHERS

Pioneering Pathways To
Inner Peace

JANE NOBLE KNIGHT

Noble Knight Publishing UK

First published 2013 in UK by Noble Knight Publishing, 1 Broadbent Court, Newport, TF10 7FE.
www.thepilgrimmother.com

ISBN: 978-0-9575262-2-8
All the information, concepts, skills, techniques and advice contained within this publication are of general comment only and are not intended in any way for any individual. The intent is to offer a variety of information and circumstances to provide a wider range of choices now and in the future, recognising that we all have widely diverse circumstances and viewpoints. Should any reader choose to make use of the information contained herein, this is their decision, and the interviewees (and their companies), the author and publisher do not assume any responsibility whatsoever under any conditions or circumstances. It is recommended that the reader obtain their own independent advice.

Cover Art "Mother Moon Mandala" courtesy of Nirjala Tamrakar Wright. This is how Nirjala describes her work: "The mandala represents Eternal Power. Within the mandala there is the Moon which represents coolness and calm and is therefore the colour blue. The Moon is also the reason for tides and waves in the ocean, which represent the ups and downs in life that women face successfully. That is why women are the strongest of all." (www.facebook.com/dannirjala.wright)

To my parents, Bob and Eunice Noble, for their long life genes and starting me off on my pilgrim's journey through life.

Foreword

June 2013

If you are scanning this book and are wondering whether to buy it then I do encourage you to do so. I felt honoured to be asked by Jane to write the foreword, and in order to do her Pilgrim Mother project justice I asked her for the chapters so that I could skim through as I was departing for an overseas trip. It was impossible to skim, for once I had started looking through the stories of the nine women, I was hooked, drawn in by the depth of their sharing and their willingness to be so open, vulnerable and completely authentic. I couldn't put the book down, so a quick, brief writing assignment turned into a much bigger project as I churned over the insights and wisdom I was gleaning ... filling my head with the lives of these incredible women and seeing what an important service they have done in telling us about their journeys.

One of the things that I am really passionate about is hosting Women's Gatherings, and as I travel overseas for more than half the year, I get to do this all over the globe. I meet women from all walks of life and learn a great deal from their different backgrounds. What I have discovered is that women the world over are inspired by the stories and personal sharing of other women. It's not so much the successes they have had that inspire us, for in fact we can be quite intimidated by some alpha women's high-rolling megastardom as they reach the heights of corporate life or win amazing prizes or awards. What we really appreciate are the details ... Why did they do what they did? How did it happen? Who did they become in the process? We even love the minutiae of their lives to be revealed so that we can say, "I do that as well" or "I know that feeling."

In many cases, when the layers are revealed, we realise just how alike we are or we see that those women have risen above challenges so much greater than the pains we have suffered, and so we know that so much more is possible for us if we dare to move forward. We don't need to let anything hold us back. I think by engaging with women like these here and connecting through these pages, you will feel encouraged with wherever you are on your own journey.

This book is full of stories and wisdom that will give you the permission or validation you may be seeking (consciously or unconsciously) to step to the next level, or perhaps allow yourself to think bigger than you have been thinking. I am speaking to you now as a woman who wants more from life and who feels you have so much to give. I am guessing that for all you have achieved so far, and perhaps overcome, you are in actual fact only just beginning.

Here I am in Bali on a Sunday morning, overwhelmed with notes and jottings from my own reading of this book and now wondering what to write. I decided to ask for guidance to give me clarity. You probably do this yourself if, like me, you have learned over the years to ask for help. So I am sitting in a cafe in Ubud reading the Jakarta Post newspaper and I see a big picture of Latino-American artist Jennifer Lopez and read her words, *"We're realising, the world is realising, that women are not even coming into their own until they are in their forties, that they have so much to offer."* As J-Lo herself approaches her mid-forties she is absolutely right with noticing this: so a big high-five to her this morning for highlighting one of the key messages that come through the stories of the nine women in Jane Noble Knight's book.

Women have so much potential inside them that is bursting to shift out in the world and be expressed in some new creative form. The urgency of this is often keenly felt by women who have moved through the early years of family-centric home-making, often juggling career, business and community commitments too, and many are now looking to a future filled with blanks and questions but very often excitement and hope as they embrace this new uncertainty. A different kind of woman is emerging now in later life. Instead of us feeling that we have a few more miles on the clock, we are trading in those tired odometers and fitting new ones to give ourselves a completely fresh start ... for some that means post-children, post-marriage, post-profession ... even post home-owning as more women uproot themselves and set off into their second 'youth' on 'gap years' and sabbatical journeys of re-invention. I think Marianne Williamson even refers to this mid-life phase as a second puberty.

There used to be three ages for women: maiden, mother and crone ... and for sure, none of us over forty resonate with that dreadful word 'crone', an aged woman who is ignored and made irrelevant by society today. So we are choosing and embracing many different rites of passage and evolving into the kind of women you will read about here ... pioneers of a new world ... This time it's not the new lands of America that we are discovering and creating; it is a new humanity. This is a new era of Pilgrim Mothers. And I would be wrong to suggest that this is solely the territory of older women. You will read here about young women who choose very different paths and push back against cultural pressure in order to forge new avenues for other young women to follow.

Jane Noble Knight is indeed doing sacred work here by celebrating the triumphs and recoveries over trauma, terrible misfortune, invisibility, heartbreak and loss in a way that these women could not. Even if they did feel moved to blow their own trumpets, that's just not the feminine way! The job for all of us is to celebrate each other, give each other a hand up, cheerlead, support and do everything we can to make visible the work of women all over the globe who are making this world a better place.

The timeliness of this book is perfect. Take a look at any TV screen or newspaper and you will see story after story that reaffirms how much humanity has lost its way. Women are missing from so much of the power-broking and decision-making forums, particularly the highest levels of government, corporations and financial institutions. We need fresh input and new energy. Women have that. We need to step forward out of the shadows with our Pilgrim energy and be prepared to make a difference and take on anything that we feel passionate about. If you need any inspiration with that then just read the wonderful stories of these nine women. I guarantee that by the end of the book you will want to do more or take the seed of the idea you have and breathe new life into it with greater confidence knowing that anything is possible.

Congratulations Jane ... I value the friendship that we have forged during our conversations about Pilgrim Mothers. Thank you for including me in your first book – that was an honour indeed. From being associated and connected with the other women in that edition, I have myself grown into another flowering of my own potential.

Gina Lazenby (from the Hub in Ubud, Bali)
CEO and Founder 'Women Gathering Project', Co-founder Feng Shui Society UK, Author of The Rise of the Feminine
www.ginalazenby.wordpress.com

Contents

"This is my story and it's time to tell it along with those of other women. … My story is intertwined with the stories of the other women in this book and, in reality, with all women. There's something that women understand without words. Maybe it's our biology, our hard wiring, our personal history; I'm not sure. All I know is that the women I meet now are very much an integral part of my journey."

JANE NOBLE KNIGHT
THE PILGRIM MOTHER

Introduction

Jane Noble Knight

Hello. I'm Jane Noble Knight. I was born a Noble and married a Knight. Strange as it may sound, it took me some time to feel comfortable with my own name … although I suppose it was really a symptom of me not feeling at home with *myself*.

When I was growing up as Jane Noble, I can remember being slightly embarrassed and intimidated by my name. It seemed too grand, too posh, too 'big' for me somehow. My mother used to say to me, "Jane Noble is a lovely name," but I wasn't convinced. I wasn't sure of what being 'noble' had to do with *me*, so I never fully inhabited my name. So when I met my husband, a 'Knight', I cheerfully jettisoned Noble and became straightforward Jane Knight. I could manage that somehow. I liked the idea of knights on a mission, seekers after truth and 'righters of wrongs'.

It was not until several decades later that I began to flirt with the idea of being a Noble Knight. In the late nineties I had come through a challenging time with my husband's ME (myalgic encephalomyelitis – also known as chronic fatigue syndrome) and over the years had just lost all notion of who I was – if I had ever really known. I wanted to get some sense of *who* I was, where I 'fitted', not just *what* I was – wife, mother, daughter, colleague, and so on.

So I started exploring my family history to see if that might shed any light on who I was. Around this time I had to set up a limited company for my earnings as a freelance Training Consultant in order to satisfy new Inland Revenue rules. I toyed with various names, as one does, and decided on Noble Knight Associates Limited. And so the Noble Knight name was birthed into the world – but at that stage only as the company's name, not mine.

I began to look at where I'd come from and whether there were any clues in my ancestors. Perhaps I had similar traits to other women in my lineage. Who knew what I might find? I did indeed chat to older family members and find stories of women in my ancestry who had been entrepreneurs, travellers, farmers, property investors, extras in the film industry and more … but those are for another time.

In 2001 I had the opportunity to delve more seriously into my family background when I had a few months enforced break between interim training contracts. One of the handed down stories particularly intrigued me. Over the years my mother had mentioned my great-uncle, John (known as Jack) Bellis, who had supposedly been shot dead by a jealous lover. She suggested he might have been seeing another woman. It was time to find out more. The research proved fascinating. By chance Jack's death had occurred in the same month as Queen Victoria's funeral in January 1901, so my gaze would be distracted and I'd end up reading all the other stories too that told of a bygone age, never to return. On another level, however, newspaper articles were full of death, distress and grief – much like now.

Jack's was one of many tragic stories in the papers. However, with my family connection it was especially poignant for me – and more complex than I had imagined. On a visit to my Auntie Amy's home in Mold, North Wales, where I had spent my first eight years, I had once seen Jack's photo of him standing alone outside his family's ironmongers' shop on the town's High Street. He was a handsome, slim young man with dark, straight hair combed back and a neat moustache. He looked very smart in his white shirt, dark trousers and starched white apron. I could imagine him turning a few girls' heads, although from later accounts that I read he was a sensible, well-liked chap.

As a boy Jack moved down to London with his brother, Edward, and when he was old enough, worked as an assistant in the hardware shop belonging to his auntie and uncle, George and Alice Griffiths, in Penton Street, Pentonville, London. Here he met Maud Amelia Eddington, who lived with her silversmith father and family in nearby Amwell Street. George and Alice moved back to North Wales for a time, leaving Jack assisting another manager before, in 1900, moving to an 'oil-shop' in Fleet Street, Hampstead, where George made Jack his shop manager. I wonder whether Jack was able to see Maud more easily when his relatives were in Wales. However, his social life, according to the newspaper articles, seemed to revolve around Sunday evenings at the Welsh Tabernacle Chapel at Charing Cross, and there was no suggestion of impropriety. So he was hardly a 'bad boy'. The move to Hampstead couldn't have helped the relationship nor the fact that Jack's Auntie Alice clearly did not like Maud.

Whatever the reason, the relationship cooled on Jack's side but not on Maud's. Tragically, on the fateful day of 14 January 1901, the heartbroken Maud, armed with a gun she had bought supposedly as a gift for a friend going to South Africa, entered the shop where Jack was working alone. Maud intended to shoot herself in front of him, but in the ensuing struggle as Jack tried to wrest the weapon from her, was fatally wounded in the head. He never regained consciousness and died later in the Hampstead Home Hospital, aged only twenty-four.

Maud was tried in the Old Bailey and found innocent of the 'wilful murder' of Jack Bellis, but guilty of 'feloniously attempting to murder herself' and was sentenced to fifteen months' hard labour in Holloway Prison. In the 1911 census I found Maud single and living in her parents' home. I was left with a sense of tragic loss – for everyone involved.

As I investigated Jack's story, I wondered how he might have felt about the way the truth of his tragic end had not been passed on to future generations. Maud too protested in court about being described as a 'singer' in the newspapers, which was totally untrue. How do these false stories occur? Maybe it's a simple case of mishearing or misconstruing information. I am particularly careful when writing to check whether the meaning I am intending is being communicated as clearly as possible. Printed words can lack the nuances that one can give to spoken words. I have deliberately used transcripts for the chapters in my books because I want each woman to speak in her own words and not give my interpretation of them.

Another reason for misunderstandings to arise is omission. My mother repeated to me how my grandmother, Jack's sister Mary, and great-grandmother Sarah had never spoken of his death. Over the years the silence of my great-grandmother appears to have been misinterpreted by other relatives. Lack of information turned the story into shame at him leading on a young woman and so another corrupted version evolved, whereas another interpretation could be that Jack's mother was grief-stricken and could not bear to mention his name ever after.

I wondered how Jack would have shared his own account of what happened … had he been afforded the opportunity. I would have loved to talk with Maud and all the family members involved in the tragedy. I was not able to do that, but I was able to rewrite Jack's story from the 1901 accounts.

Unbeknownst to me at the time, I was to come across another story in January 2010 whose truth had been lost in history. I had called in the services of intuitive business mentor, Katharine Dever, whose story is told in my first book.[a] At the time I had a very strong feeling I was meant to be doing something with my life, but despite my best endeavours I couldn't quite grasp what it was. I couldn't seem to arrange all my jigsaw pieces into a fully completed picture. It reminded me of the Morecambe and Wise sketch where Mr 'Preview' (André Previn) told Eric Morecambe that he was playing all the wrong notes, to which Eric responded that in fact he was playing all the *right* notes … but not necessarily in the right order! Katharine helped me put my notes in the right order.[1]

With Katharine's help I recognised that my mission was connected with the story of the Pilgrim Mothers. This phrase had been in my head for nine months, but I hadn't realised its significance till then. I had heard of the Pilgrim Fathers who sailed to the US from the UK in the *Mayflower* in 1620, but I assumed it was men who made the trip, as I had never heard any women mentioned.

It was only after Katharine visited me that I began to research the Pilgrim Mothers' story. I discovered they were amazing pioneering women, part of whose story is told in Sue Allan's chapter. Like Jack Bellis, their story had been lost. Through Sue's retelling, their lives are once more coming to life.

In *The Inspiring Journeys* series I want to share stories just like these that might otherwise be lost or known only to a handful of people. I believe the stories deserve a wider audience and readership.

In this second book I want to give a voice to nine women I have met on my own personal pilgrimage. These conversations were recorded between March 2012 and June 2013. I am keen that every one of these women's fascinating stories be shared from their own personal perspective, using their own words, without either my own or anyone else's subsequent interpretation.

I call these women modern Pilgrim Mothers. I want to share and celebrate their lives – and those of other pioneers. Women have a tendency to be overly modest. On the whole we are uncomfortable singing our own praises. It feels like bragging. Men are much more willing to shout out about how great they are, whether others agree with them or not.

I believe there's a happy medium. If women don't celebrate their successes, they remain hidden and we need women role models. *Visible* role models. So how do we overcome women's reticence?

Well, first of all, women have to be prepared to tell their stories. We all have them. What we may regard as uninteresting is actually extremely interesting to others who might be facing similar challenges. I applaud the women in this book for sharing their stories. From my own experience I know it takes courage.

Secondly, women need to get used to accepting praise and compliments without deflecting them. That was a tough one for me. I started by saying, "Thank you. That's very kind of you," when paid a compliment and step by step began to feel easier accepting thanks and recognition instead of brushing it to one side.

Thirdly, I have observed that it is easier to let others celebrate us than for us to celebrate

---

1   Much loved British comic double act, working in variety, radio, film and most successfully in television. This sketch from their 1971 Christmas Show is one of the most famous.

ourselves. So let's get singing the praises of women we know whenever we can. This book is my contribution.

Maybe women will then become accustomed to speaking, still with humility and yet without embarrassment about our successes.

So thank you to all the fabulous women in this book … and to all the amazing women who will be appearing in future books … and to all the wonderful women I may never meet but who every day are making a difference to those around them.

As I have finally stepped into my own name as a Noble Knight by sharing some of my stories and these women's, so have these modern Pilgrim Mothers also stepped out into the world to proclaim who they are.

Join me in celebrating their lives …

AMANDA REED

"When I'm rejected, I always think, 'Well, actually, that now leaves my life completely open for anything else to drop into it...'"

photo courtesy of Claire Grogan

Amanda Reed was born and bred in Birmingham, UK, but spent most of her life in beautiful Shropshire. Since the moment she made the audience laugh in the school play, all she wanted to be when she grew up was an actress. But the parents had other ideas. "Get yourself a career to fall back on," they said. So, two marriages, two children, two divorces and two careers later ... she finally threw in the towel and surrendered to her dream. She graduated drama school in 2002 and has not stopped working since.

Amanda played in the Royal National Theatre's production of Alan Bennett's *The History Boys*. Her West End credits include another Alan Bennett play, *Enjoy*, and J.B. Priestley's *When We Are Married*. December 2012 saw her first appearance on TV in the BBC's *Doctors*. She is now looking to add more TV and film to her growing list of credits. Amanda is currently appearing in Terence Rattigan's *Less Than Kind*. Amanda lives in Wimbledon, London – home of Championship Tennis and The Wombles.

www.amanda-reed.co.uk

A Conversation with Amanda Reed

Twilight Star

How many friends have you connected with first on social media sites before meeting them face-to-face? Douglas is one such friend. Knowing from our conversations that I was a huge fan of Alison Steadman, Douglas invited me to *Enjoy*, Alan Bennett's revived play, starring the great actor herself. He bought, literally, the last two opening night tickets, single seats rows apart. Now Douglas very cleverly combines his love of photography and drama by supplying his local press with photos of theatre productions. As a 'Friend' of Nottingham Playhouse, he invited me to 'meet the cast' after the performance. Woohoo! I couldn't wait.

When the evening arrived, I sat enthralled by Alison's aging 'Mam' as she faced the onset of Alzheimer's Disease. After the cast's standing ovation, I made my way upstairs against the flow of people, feeling excited and apprehensive. I was expecting far more fans than I found in the bar area, so my spirits rose at the possibility I might actually get to say hello to my heroine!

As I observed cast members and crew arriving, a woman of similar age and height to me appeared at my side, smiling warmly, and introduced herself as Amanda. Her fine, dark blonde, straight hair was cut in a short twenties style fringed bob, which showed off her sparkling, expressive eyes to perfection. Not everyone suits that severe style, but it looked great on Amanda. I learned that she was the understudy for Alison as Connie/Mam and for Carol McCready as Mrs Clegg. As Amanda shared snippets of her story, I was so fascinated I arranged to go back and record a conversation with her three days later.

It was Amanda who spotted Alison arriving first. I turned to see my long time icon surrounded by a growing queue of autograph hunters. Amanda commented, "You know, they just get Alison to sign their programme, but she loves to chat about the play and her work." Armed with that nugget, as the queue subsided and Amanda went to mingle elsewhere, I made my way over to meet Alison, remarking how she looked more like her usual glamorous self, to which she smiled, "I couldn't have come up to meet people as Mam!"

I was enthralled for twenty minutes, chatting about the play, her realistic wig that reminded me of my nana's hairdo, Twinkie home perms, her hometown of Liverpool and my university town.

As we reminisced I was stunned to discover that, as a student, I had actually experienced one of Alison's first performances at the Everyman Theatre in John McGrath's *Soft or a Girl*. I remembered a particularly memorable scene featuring Alison, but I had not realised till now that it was her. Before Alison moved on, she wrote in my programme, 'To Jane, thanks for being a great fan, Alison Steadman.' Wow!!

Now three days later, I am back to have a conversation with Amanda, this time not as an understudy but as the first 'star' of my collection of modern Pilgrim Mothers in my Inspiring Journeys series. Armed with my brand new camcorder and one practice run under my belt, I arrive early in Nottingham to buy a tripod and spare memory cards.

With a few minutes to spare I make my way to the stage door. Amanda comes tripping along in her bubbly fashion a minute later. She has a spare hour before a rehearsal. I follow her up a few flights of metallic stairs, our footsteps echoing loudly. What a contrast to the rather plush front of house. It reminds me of a functional warehouse – a large, uncarpeted space.

Amanda shows me into a long, narrow, rather bare dressing room with a wall of rectangular mirrors, each topped by unforgiving light bulbs. Nevertheless, the room feels welcoming, lit by Amanda's warm presence and a vase of happy sunflowers...

I can't wait to hear your story from the snippets I've heard so far, Amanda. Where shall we start?

How long have you got? *[Laughing]* I'll speak quickly because there's a lot to tell. So I'll give you the précis ... I left school at eighteen, didn't get into university and wasn't *allowed* to apply to drama school. (Parents didn't want me to go and I couldn't fight City Hall, unfortunately.) I went into the Navy as a Wren for fifteen months, where I met my first husband. We married and went to live in Malta for two years. I had my first child there. I spent the next ten years being a wife and mother.

Came back to the UK. Had another child and really just lost the dream. I'd always wanted to be an actor, all my life. And I just got to the point at age thirty-five where I thought, *I'm not going to do this now. I'm going to have to put this one to bed and forget about it because if I was meant to be an actor, it would have happened by now, and I would have done something about it.*

So I worked as a primary school teacher for almost nine years. Then I fancied a change. I'd only picked being a teacher because it fitted in with the girls' school hours and holidays. So I became a financial consultant for eleven years on a salary, not a commission-only, hungry basis. And found myself two marriages, two divorces, two children and two careers later, doing the washing up one day and thinking if I sold my house and gave my job up and sold everything I own, liquidated my pension and my savings, I could afford to go to drama school! The kids had left home. I didn't have to ask for anybody's permission.

So that's exactly what I did. I applied to drama school, was accepted straight away, sold my house almost immediately and everything just slotted into place. So off I went to drama school for a one-year postgrad course in Birmingham.

Was there a defining moment?

[Reflecting] There was really. I'd lost a dear friend recently who'd left me a little money, so I was dreaming about what to do with it. I'd just cooked dinner for another friend, Neil, and he suggested, "Well, haven't you always wanted to be an actor?" And I'd actually forgotten. It was the last thing on my mind. And I thought, *Yes. You're right.* So I put the wheels in motion – that must have been May – and by the first week in June I'd got a place at drama school. It was that quick. And in September I started and my house was sold and everything I'd owned had gone. And then I was in one room with a suitcase. It was a big leap.

Twelve months later, I found myself touring with *Brief Encounter*. I did absolutely everything – Assistant Stage Manager, Wardrobe Mistress, washed and ironed all the costumes, understudied two main roles, had a little part of my own, helped assemble the set, pull it down after the end of each week … I was exhausted by the end. *But* I did get to go on as one of the characters I was understudying and do her role for six months. So, it was a wonderful training ground.

When I was in insurance, there was a manager who inspired me. He gave me lots of tips such as: To achieve your goal you've got to break it down into steps and decide what you're going to sacrifice to get there. I sacrificed everything. I literally burned all my boats and jumped.

Twelve months later, I was touring in Leeds when he called me. "I've just seen you in *Brief Encounter*. You inspire *me*, Amanda Reed."

"Well," I replied, "I jumped and the parachute opened."

"That's what minds and parachutes have in common; they only work when they're open."

So he was very instrumental in me having the courage to do what I wanted to do.

Then there was a dry spell of about three years without any paid work. I thought, *Oh dear, is that it then?* So, during that period, I did a lot of unpaid work: short films; fringe theatre; getting to know the ins and outs of the theatre; how to work an audience; do a variety of different characters; add things to my CV; and hone my craft.

> "I sacrificed everything. I literally burned all my boats and jumped."

So when I was asked to understudy Maureen Lipman and Lesley Dunlop in *Martha, Josie and the Chinese Elvis*, I thought, *Yes, I can do that.* It was a big undertaking. They were never off the stage. That led to understudying Mrs Lintott in *The History Boys* tour.

I really love the stage. It's my first love. I've always just wanted to do play after play after play, even though it's not as well paid as other things. I played one of the little old ladies in *Arsenic and Old Lace* at the Vienna English Theatre for nine weeks. As a lead actor I got to go on every night and make the audience laugh. You can really hone your craft and learn what works, what doesn't and why not. We had some difficult audiences and some wildly appreciative audiences, especially the Vienna Boys' Choir who came for a matinee. Hundreds of them filled the theatre and gave us a standing ovation with football whistles, shouts, whoops and shrieks as if we'd just scored a goal. It was brilliant. They were great fun.

Then Chris Luscombe, Director of *Enjoy*, asked me to understudy Mam and Mrs Clegg, which I've been doing for nearly two years.

You're understudying for two fantastic women's roles. What are the challenges of Alison Steadman's Mam role?

Mam really runs the gamut of emotions. She's got the beginnings of Alzheimer's, so that's an added challenge to really get the variety. Mam changes on a minute-by-minute basis. She reacts differently to every word. Chris Luscombe refers to it as 'turning on a sixpence'. I watch how Alison turns on the sixpence. In the same speech she'll be three different people. I really love that. I've learned a great deal to add to my repertoire too.

As the understudy, do you need to be similar or bring your own spin to it?

A bit of both, really. You're expected to make the moves exactly the same; deliver the lines in a similar way. But I couldn't possibly do what Alison's doing. Alison is Alison and I'm me. It would end up a really poor impersonation and we want her to look real when she's on stage. That's what I try and do, although I've never been called on as an understudy in two years. But all the understudies performed to an invited audience of 500 in the West End last year. Acting's a two-way thing. It's impossible to get the best out of the play with a non-receptive audience. As understudies, you rehearse without an audience you can interact with, so you never know their reaction till you're on stage.

Do you dread or relish stepping in?

Twelve months ago, I'd have said I had a bit of dread. But after the fantastic reception from the West End audience, it's laid the ghost. Now, if I get called on, I'll love it. I know I can do this – without wishing for anything terrible to happen, of course!

I'm amazed how you learn all the lines.

The rehearsal process involves you thinking through why you're saying something. Each line is a piece of the jigsaw, and it's a massive jigsaw in this case. The main actors get the chance to work it through together with the director.

An understudy has to learn those lines cold, basically. That's the difficult thing for me. I'd once said to someone, "I hate learning by rote," and they responded, "Don't learn it by rote; learn it by heart." They were so right. You don't just parrot the lines if you listen to the relay every night of the show so that it absorbs into your psyche, almost by osmosis.

This script is a challenge. In the beginning it was absolute hell. Mam has Alzheimer's. She repeats herself a lot, *but* every time she says it in a slightly different way. If you say it in the wrong way, the person gives you the wrong line back and then everybody loses their place in the play. You have to memorise it, absolutely perfectly.

> "I'd once said to someone, 'I hate learning by rote,' and they responded, 'Don't learn it by rote; learn it by heart.'"

I'd sit there thinking, *I can't remember the next line.* And the line would be "I can't remember. My mother was like that." So your head's telling you "I can't remember," but the line is "I can't remember." It really did my head in.

But Alison said it's the hardest thing she's ever had to learn, too, after forty years' experience.

That's quite encouraging. *[Laughing]* It's not just my inexperience or incompetence!

I'd like to have my own understudy one day. And I would be really nice to her like they are to me. *[Laughing]*

I'm sure you would be. So who inspires you?

Alison Steadman. She adds so much to her character and the rich language that Alan Bennett provides her with. She works very, very hard at her trade and she inspires me greatly. Alison says it's all luck, but I would say it's talent.

Another one is Judi Dench. All my life people have said I look like her. So I watch everything she does. She played Titania at seventy-four; and Siân Phillips at eighty-plus has been Juliet in *Romeo and Juliet*, set in an Old People's Home. So I've lots to look forward to.

Is the theatre bucking the trend of television and using older women in roles traditionally written for younger women?

There are lots of older women at the forefront. I think it's good that it's been highlighted because it has made directors and producers think carefully about representing the whole female population. We are an aging society. Over sixties are going to be something like fifty percent of the population within ten years. That's a lot of people. I know it's a cliché, but age is just a number. It's what you make of your age and your experience that matters.

> "Age is just a number. It's what you make of your age and your experience that matters."

So it's a very exciting time for women over fifty, and as far as acting is concerned, there are some fantastic roles for older women. If beautiful, lead actresses attain the age of forty or forty-five and think they've had it, it's very sad. I don't have that problem because even if I'd gone into acting when I was fifteen, I would have never been a young female lead – the young beautiful ingénue. My face tells everybody I'm a character actor, with a lot of comedy attached. But there are lots of roles for people my age, as I've proven. Every time I turn around, there's another one, which is lovely.

That's a really interesting perspective. What would you say to anyone with a dream, whatever it may be?

There will be a time in your life when, if you look carefully at the circumstances around you, you could do it. You'll never miss the opportunity. You can always create another one. But having the courage to do it is a different thing. Now this may seem rather strange, but I didn't even think about how difficult it was going to be. I didn't think about what I was going to lose in doing so; I didn't think twice about selling all my belongings and downsizing to one room. It was just something I needed to do in order to get to where I wanted to go. Whether it's to climb Everest, sail singlehandedly around the world or do voluntary services overseas, whatever it is you want to do, you have to give up things. You have to sacrifice things. If you're prepared to do that then you can have your dream.

It's whether or not you grasp the opportunities with both hands. If you're the sort of person who is timid and frightened about things then you really have to put it behind you. That's all that's between you and your dream. If you're not prepared to do it then dream about something else.

You've taken what many people would regard as considerable risks, Amanda.

You have too, I think. You've gone down a completely untrodden path, haven't you, Jane, with this project of yours?

Yes, I have, and I had absolutely no option but to do it. I couldn't *not* do it. A bit like you felt, Amanda. You learn as you go along.

What have you learned in your life, Amanda?

Millions of things. I haven't had an easy life. I often think of what I would do if I won the lottery. But I don't need to. I'm perfectly happy where I am, doing what I'm doing. What on earth would you do with unlimited money? There'd be nothing for you to go for. There's a huge sense of achievement when you succeed. I had to work hard, virtually brought the kids up on my own and lived most of my life in a council house in Telford with very little. It was a tough existence; one time I just had a bed and cooker. But because of that, because I know what it's like to have absolutely nothing, I'm not afraid of going back there. I've had times in my life where I've been really depressed, very upset. I mean, divorce does terrible things to you.

[Pointing out the sunflowers in the vase] Sunflowers are my motif. Nothing to do with *Calendar Girls*, I hasten to add. I did NLP – Neuro-Linguistic Programming – on myself and I literally only have to see the colour yellow now and it always brings a smile to my face.

So you've really got to build your inner resources and make sure that you're as mentally healthy as possible. Then whatever's thrown at you, you can jump off and grasp the opportunities with both hands. It's a scary thing to do.

> "… you've really got to build your inner resources … Then whatever's thrown at you, you can jump off and grasp the opportunities with both hands."

Indeed. I've likened it to the Indiana Jones film where he puts his foot out into the abyss and the path comes up to meet it. There's definitely something about just going for it.

There's a Popeye cartoon where the baby Swee'Pea goes crawling off on a building site; he crawls onto the lift and the lift takes him up and he keeps crawling up; he crawls off the lift onto a girder; and the girder comes up and takes him. My friend said, "Life's like that. You just need to move and something will come along and take you."

I love that. I remember that Swee'Pea cartoon.

And your heart's in your mouth and he just keeps crawling. You think he will just fall, but then along comes that girder and off he goes.

I've recently read a book called *The Decisive Moment* by Jonah Lehrer. It explains how we make snap decisions. When I met you in the bar the other night after the show, I don't know what made me turn and speak to you. There was just something about you. You're not on anyone's radar when you're an understudy. I could have either taken my drink and sat down quietly until somebody from the cast joined me, *or* I could have made an effort. I looked at you and immediately spoke. I don't know what made me do that. But *The Decisive Moment* says we take in billions of signals whenever we look at anything, whenever we hear anything. The atmosphere in a room, all sorts of things, all play on our senses and our instinct tells us exactly what to do. Sometimes we override and rationalise it too much. *They'll think I'm a nutter if I speak now.* Then the opportunity is gone. If you act on your instinct, you never know what might come of it.

I do the same when I'm walking around a strange town, as I do a lot. I let my feet take me into a bookshop, a clothes shop, a café – wherever – I don't worry where or why. I'm not on a mission. Some of the people I've met, things I've seen, places I've been by allowing myself that luxury, are just amazing. I keep a little journal to record anything unusual or strange or different that happens to me. There's a lot of understudy dressing room time I've wasted the last three years, so I've started writing a play and incorporating all these little observations. We'll see whether anything comes of it. I suppose that's my next project.

> "If you act on your instinct, you never know what might come of it."

Fantastic. I often think writing something down creates its own momentum and brings dreams into reality.

That's right; something strange happens. Your perception is immortalised in black and white on a page, whereas if you leave it a few weeks or six months, your perception's completely different. And in the process of writing it down, you also start to think around the subject in between, beneath and beyond the lines and all that embeds itself in your writing as well. When I read back through my little notebook, I think, *I'd forgotten that happened. That was an amazing thing. Is that what I thought of it then?* Because when I think back, that's not how I feel about it. And we're weird creatures, aren't we? The way the brain plays tricks on us and what we think happened didn't necessarily happen. That's another story as they say. We could go off in a completely different direction there, couldn't we? …

I catch up with Amanda two years later by phone. She is a person I want to keep in touch with very much…

When we last met, you were understudying Alison Steadman, with a few more weeks still to go with that run. What happened after that, Amanda?

Good question. What always happens after the end of a show is – you panic. You try and get some part-time or temping work, which I did. Actually, I managed to persuade a company that I wanted a real job. I trained as a House, Contents and Buildings Insurance expert. This was like a permanent, long-term career move, really. So, it was quite lucrative, unlike most temping jobs. I said it would be at least six months before I got another job. I think I was with them all of two months before I said, "I'm really sorry, but I've got another job. I can't turn this one down." They weren't very pleased, but they knew the deal when I started with them.

Strangely, I had received a call from my agent who said, "You've been called to do a role."

I said, "What? No audition? Anything?"

"No, no, they really, really want you. It's in the West End, not touring."

"Who's called me?"

It was Chris Luscombe who'd directed *Enjoy*. He wanted me to join a star-studded list of comedy actors, like Roy Hudd and Sam Kelly, in *When We Are Married* by J B Priestley. My agent told me, "You'll be understudying Maureen Lipman and Lynda Baron if you decide to take it."

I was thrilled to bits to be asked. So that was a nice, long run in the West End from September 2009 until February 2010. Actually, we started with two weeks in Guildford. We'd had a bit of an argument with the production company because they wouldn't let the understudies sit in on rehearsals. They wanted the understudies just to join in the West End. Technically, if you are stationary in a place, for insurance purposes, the production company doesn't need to employ understudies. However, in reality, if anything happened, they would be required to go on, probably with the book, but you don't know where you're moving on the stage, how the play works, what people are doing. Nothing. So, it's very, very hard. Anyway, we managed to persuade them we needed to sit in on rehearsals for at least two of the four weeks and they let us do that, which was very lucky because in Week 2, in Guildford, Lynda Baron went off with an eye problem. She was off for two performances. We'd still had no rehearsals, but we'd watched rehearsals. So I had to go on.

How much notice did you have?

Probably about forty-five minutes.

Amanda, what on earth did you feel like?

Well, you can't allow yourself to panic, you see. You have to be ice-cold because if I had actually allowed myself to feel the feelings that I wanted to feel at that point, I would never have gone on. So I just took it in my stride and asked, "Okay, what do we have to do?" All the main cast came piling in to help me rehearse. I was in five little scenes, but one of them was the main denouement, without which the whole play would have been pointless. Nobody would have understood what on earth was going on.

It was a huge responsibility. I do admit to having dried at one point, but Maureen Lipman and Susie Blake, out of the kindness of their hearts, bailed me out. It was fine after that. But dear, oh dear!

> "… you can't allow yourself to panic … if I had actually allowed myself to feel the feelings that I wanted to feel at that point, I would never have gone on."

What was the audience's reaction to you? That must always be a concern when you're an understudy for a big name.

It was. When I went on for Alison in *Enjoy*, the whole audience groaned. They'd come all that way just to see her. But with nine excellent comedy actors in this play, if one went off at least you got all the others. And yes, it's sad they didn't see Lynda Baron for those two performances, but they had Maureen and Roy and Michelle Dotrice. It was a lovely, lovely play and I learnt so much watching these amazing people.

They were very understanding, and you always get a special round of applause when you go on the first time. So that was nice as well.

Are there any stories you can share from working with so many big name actors?

There's a kind of rule that what goes on tour stays on tour. And yes, there are some outrageous things that happen. I will tell you one little story. I had to go on for Maureen when we went to the West End. It was almost at the end of the run. She was really poorly and struggled all week, convinced she'd be able to get through Saturday's matinee and evening performances. And Maureen never goes off. When I understudied her before on a huge, long tour, she never had one day off. But on the Saturday morning she phoned, and I had a great time understudying her in those two performances.

On the Monday, there was a gift carrier bag on my dressing table with a little card from Maureen, thanking me very much. Inside was a silver, long cardboard box. I thought, *Oh, this looks nice. It might be perfume or something.* I took it out and looked at it and read 'Cellulite Cream.' You never know whether she's just being a bit eccentric or whether it's a kind of playful dig. I ran down the six flights of stairs and knocked on the door and I said, "Hi, are you feeling better, Maureen?"

She said, "Oh yes I am, thank you, Amanda. Thanks so much for going on for me."

I said, "Thank you for your lovely present. Just what I needed."

I didn't wait to see her face. I just ran out. You get to expect that kind of thing from Maureen. She's got a heart of gold, but she has these little quirks and foibles. I've still got it. Unused. I feel like framing it. Maybe I shall raffle it.

Then in the first week we joined the rehearsal in the West End, I had a text from my sister. My mum had had a fall and she'd gone into hospital in Newark, Nottinghamshire. I thought, *Oh dear.* She was getting on. During the whole of the run, Mum got progressively worse until finally she went into a care home.

When I knew she was dying, I had another brief text from my sister: "Better get up here quick. She's not expected to last and they won't resuscitate." I then phoned the care home and the hospital to get more information from the horse's mouth, so to speak, because the information coming through was a bit scant. I felt awful. And all the while, I was still in this play.

So, I'm sitting in Kings Cross Station on December 14th at 6:30 at night, even though I've got the message mid-morning, waiting for my company manager to tell me whether she could allow me to go up to Newark or whether I have to get on the Northern Line back down to the theatre because somebody was ill.

Of course, when you're a main cast person, if something happens, the understudy goes on. But if you're the understudy and you're covering two people, you can't go. So I sat there, waiting for this phone call. I phoned them in the end. "Oh, yes, it's all right, you can go." I jumped on the next train and went straight up to Newark. I was just in time. She died about twenty minutes after I got there. It was as if she had been waiting for me, you know.

Then I came back from the funeral, January 11th, and had to go on the following day as understudy. That's what you have to do, you see.

> "… you learn to split yourself into two different people – the work person and the private person."

So it was a very, very upsetting time – the sort of time that really tests you and where you learn to split yourself into two different people – the work person and the private person. You just have to get on with it. So that was a bit of a challenge really, but we got through it in the end.

Is it something you've always been able to do or something you had to learn?

I think that because I was virtually a single mother – I had a husband but he was away at sea most of the time, and I had to make all the decisions for everybody all of the time … I had to run the house, look after the kids, hold down a teaching job, study an Open University degree … I never stopped – I think all of those things have to go into different compartments. I know that most actors who are in the same situation would behave in the same way.

I once read the comedian, Beryl Reid's, biography. She was a Brummie too, like we were. Strangely, my mother's name was Beryl Reed, spelt slightly differently. So Beryl the comedian was always a high profile figure in our family. That was years and years before Mum died. In fact, Mum and I were on holiday together in Menorca. When her mum died, Beryl was starring in a pantomime in Birmingham as the character, Marlene. I don't know if you ever saw her do Marlene?

Yes. I remember it well.

Anyway, Beryl's mum died and as she was star of the show, there was nobody who could cover for her because it was her stand-up routine, effectively. And she didn't go and see her dying mum and she couldn't attend the funeral. She was devastated because her mum helped her a lot. She cited the fact that her mum gave her £36,000 towards her training and to help her when she was struggling. I've always remembered that and kept it in my head because I thought there might come a time one day when I'm going to be in that situation. And sure enough, I was.

> "I was preparing myself … for a long, long time … I think that's the key in life."

I was preparing myself for it for a long, long time before it actually happened, and I think that's the key in life. If you can rehearse your situation in your head, whether you're an actor or anything else – not in a sense of worrying about what's to come but 'If this should happen, how would I behave?' – I think then when it does happen you've already rehearsed it so many times in your head that you know exactly what to do.

It's like anything really … If you're a paramedic who has to revive somebody who's had an accident on the road, you don't stand there thinking, *What on earth do I do here?* You've already done it in your head so many times that even if it's the first time you've had to do it in real life, you know exactly what to do and you get on with it. That applies to lots of different professions, doesn't it? Not just acting.

Yes, but with acting or any sort of performance, it hits home even more because it's so extreme. You have to give so much of yourself. I think it's hugely admirable.

Well, I'll tell you what, Jane … If you can't give 100 per cent of your energy and focus, your performance suffers. I'm the first to admit that I can't do it all the time. Anything could flip your concentration for a second and you're gone … and you have to get yourself back quickly. Actually, when an understudy comes on, it's really, really exciting. You've been doing a play over and over for months and months and you know it really, really well, and then you've got this unknown quantity on the stage with you. It really sharpens up everybody's performance.

You're roasting hot because of the adrenaline, and you're there in your corsets and your petticoats and your heavy, thick brocades, fanning yourself in the wings, thinking, *Oh my God. What do I do?* It's all about concentration – just getting your head in the right space, I think.

When you're performing to an audience that expects a performance and they've all paid forty-five pounds to come and see you, it's a big responsibility – one that you take on as part of the job.

Do you ever feel star-struck yourself?

All the time. When I first met Alison Steadman, I just looked into her eyes and I curtsied. "I'm really sorry," I said, "but I've admired you for so long and I've watched you in virtually everything you've ever been in and I think you're wonderful." She looked at me as if I was completely mad. Unfortunately, I can't hide my emotions. I have to say what's on my mind. In fact, somebody described it to me as having slight Tourette's. Sometimes the filter doesn't kick in, you know?

I think it's really lovely that you're so open with your emotions in that way.

Well, Alison and I got to know each other over a period of time, but she really wasn't quite sure to start with. Actually, I'm still very star-struck. Whenever I get into a play, I think, *Oh my goodness, I'm standing on stage with this person and that person* as I've watched them on the telly for so long. I think more so because I've only been acting for ten years.

Recently I had a meeting with Danny Boyle, the Director. You know, he's doing the Opening Ceremony of the Olympics. There wasn't a soul around apart from me and I wasn't expecting that at all. I didn't see him to start with. I saw his Casting Director and then his Assistant Director, who was lovely, and then they went and got him and introduced me to him. And again, I was like a goldfish.

He said, "Hello, I'm Danny." Because they do this, you know. They shake your hand as if they're just an ordinary bloke.

I said, "Yes, I know. I'm Amanda, how do you do?"

It was so, so exciting. I was absolutely bursting. By the time I came out, I wanted to tell the whole world what he wanted me to do because it was absolutely extraordinary. In my wildest dreams, I could never have thought it, you know?

> "... I'm still very star-struck ... I think, 'Oh my goodness, I'm standing on stage with this person and that person...'"

Unfortunately, ten days later it was "I'm ever so sorry. We can't do it now." Part of the project was shelved, but I had to sign an official non-disclosure form on pain of death! So I still can't tell you about it. Sorry. I would if I could!

You must have had quite a few disappointments like that. It must be the nature of the world that you live in.

You do have a lot of rejection. I'm very lucky that I don't tend to audition anymore. I just read a part of the script they're considering me for. With some, I've got the part and others have gone, "Oh no. That's not what we had in mind at all." These things happen. When I'm rejected, I always think, *Well, actually, that now leaves my life completely open for anything else to drop into it. Now is the time when Mike Leigh could phone and say, "Right, I want you in my next film and you're going to spend six months on your own in a room, thinking about your character,"* or whatever he does.

That's a wonderful attitude. So many people can't deal with rejection at all. So it's admirable that you're able to do that. I'm sure it happens as well that you create a vacuum or a door closes and something else comes along.

It's something I learnt to do when I was selling insurance all those years ago. I'd phone 100 people to get ten appointments to sell two policies. Ninety nos. It's very difficult to get ten yeses but that's the way you have to do it. You have to always work on the one-in-ten principle – you've got to apply for ten jobs to get one audition. That's an awful lot of applications.

It is, yes. I was in insurance myself. It's a tough part of the job. It's why people get paid well because not everyone can do it. They don't have that toughness.

Likewise with acting. Recently I got a tiny two-second bit in an advert for Lloyds Pharmacy. All I had to do was look out of a window and smile and wave. It was the easiest money I've ever made in my life. I thought, *Well, that wasn't bad for a day's work.* But then, it's taken me ten years to get it!

What would be your ideal role, Amanda?

I did it at the English-speaking Theatre of Frankfurt in September and October 2011. It was Lady Bracknell in Oscar Wilde's *The Importance of Being Earnest*. I had a wonderful time. I've wanted to do that role ever since I knew it existed. She's the absolute epitome of a part for me. When I was at high school, I played Gwendolyn, Lady Bracknell's headstrong daughter. I had to wait so many years because she's been played by all the 'grandes dames' of the theatre. I was actually wearing Penelope Keith's costumes, incidentally. She'd done it in the West End a couple of years prior and we hired the costumes from Angel. We had to take quite a bit off the length, put it that way, and let it out just a little round the waist. But apart from that, they were absolutely gorgeous. I'll probably do her again somewhere because age doesn't matter, as long as you're over forty. You can play her right the way till you're seventy, really.

> "Every journey starts with the first step … You just have to take the first step and the rest follows."

Well, considering you didn't get started until ten years ago, Amanda, it's absolutely amazing what you've achieved.

It's just ten years this year, actually. I amaze myself really. Every journey starts with the first step, doesn't it? You just have to take the first step and the rest follows. But sitting there wishing you had done something is the saddest thing in the world, I think. I say to my girls, I never regret any of the men I slept with, only the ones I didn't.

Tell me more.

I'll save it for the biography. I'm going to do a naughty one when I've finished writing my nice one for the girls with all the risqué bits chopped out. I'll call it somebody else's biography.

I've been trying to write chronologically. When I've checked back in my diary, I've put certain things in completely the wrong place. I love this quote from Julian Barnes' *The Sense of an Ending*:

"What you end up remembering isn't always the same as what you have witnessed." It's about revising your memory retrospectively, and it's fascinating because you can be absolutely adamant that something has happened and it either never happened at all or it happened in a completely different way.

Both your autobiographies sound like interesting reads too.

I'm writing now between acting jobs. My friend Katie used to call this in-between period 'liminal'. It's the pause at the end of the play before the audience starts clapping. It's that treading water feeling between jobs, but it can also be applied to anything, not just acting – where things could go one way or the other. I'd like to investigate it more. I can think of several liminal moments in my life where I knew my next step was going to take me off in a completely different direction. Did you ask him to put a condom on? Too late. You've had your liminal moment and you didn't grasp it. You know what I mean. It can change your whole life in a second.

It happens to us all the time but mostly we're not aware of it. Most people take risks all the time in life.

If I may, I've got a quote for you by Paulo Coelho to finish off: "Everything will be all right in the end, and if it is not all right then it is not yet the end."

What an adventurous journey Amanda has undertaken! Amanda was fifty-one when she had her second chance to live the acting dream she had discarded at thirty-five. This time she grabbed it. We always have chances to fulfil our ambitions as long as we remember the dream – or in Amanda's case, someone else does on our behalf. That's a real friend. A friend who encourages us to have adventures – not a so-called friend who holds us back.

I'm so grateful to Amanda for reminding me of the sequence with Swee'Pea on the building site in Popeye, one of my childhood favourite cartoons. I loved the way Popeye transformed into a superhero just by knocking back a can of spinach. When I was seven, I remember pestering my mum to get me some spinach so I could be like Popeye. She couldn't get any fresh spinach, so she got me some frozen spinach instead. I wasn't impressed. I couldn't believe that Popeye's food of choice was this bitter mush. There was obviously a mistake somewhere. I asked whether she could get me a can of spinach next time, convinced that was the problem. Unfortunately, cans of spinach couldn't be found anywhere, so I had to put away those thoughts of 'quick fix' magic.

Yet how many of us, especially in this Western world of speed and instant gratification, are still constantly looking for this quick fix? Dieting pills, plastic surgery, botox, beta blockers, sleeping tablets, painkillers, airbrushing … What about patience, natural cures, healthy lifestyles, moderation, looking after ourselves inside and out? I am a great believer in what shines within radiates out. I am nowhere near 'perfect' in my human body, but I can live with myself; if there's anything I really don't like about myself, whether physical or psychological, then I can work on changing it in my own way.

As I look back on the Popeye cartoon, I realise that Swee'Pea is now my idea of a superhero. An innocent at large, happy just being, trusting all will turn out well, taking life in his stride, making progress with baby steps. Surely that's the secret to life. Some may see the steps as risks, but somehow there's no alternative. I suspect the difference is when you have a sense of a calling; a feeling that you can't *not* do what's before you on your path. When you wake up to that sort of experience, life is never the same again. You just keep following the call.

Amanda certainly followed her calling to be an actor, however crazy it might have appeared to others. Amanda is now a shining star in her own life's production, as are we all if we allow ourselves to be. We each have a role to play that no one else can fulfil. As Amanda demonstrates, it doesn't matter what your age, you can start living your authentic life, the life of your most fabulous dreams, right now. Are you living your dream? I sincerely hope so. If not, what's stopping you?

"What shines within radiates out."

JANE NOBLE KNIGHT

SUE ALLAN

"I wish somebody could have said to me when I was in that really dark place ... 'The only person holding you back is yourself.' "

Sue Allan is a self-confessed history junkie! Her first book *Mayflower Maid* was published in 2004 at the age of fifty. Since then she has had four further novels published as well as four non-fiction books. Her latest is *In Search of Scrooby Manor (Domtom Publishing 2013)*. Sue also runs Mayflower Pilgrim Tours, guiding visitors around the Pilgrim sites in Lincolnshire and surrounding counties. Her great passion is Gainsborough Old Hall and its fascinating connection to the Pilgrims' story, of which she is now considered to be an expert. Sue has made numerous TV and radio appearances. She both acted as advisor and featured in the 2012 film *Monumental*, produced by and starring Hollywood actor, Kirk Cameron. Sue is a dual British–Canadian citizen. She has four sons and lives in a cosy cottage with her American partner, Roger.

www.mayflowermaid.com

A Conversation with
Sue Allan

Mayflower Maid

*H*ave you ever spoken to someone for the first time and felt as if you've known them forever? Sue was one of those people for me. I came to know her initially through an introduction by Julie Dunstan of Scrooby Manor, home of the Pilgrims Mary and William Brewster. (Third chapter) Just before Christmas 2010, I phoned Sue to introduce myself and share my interest in the Pilgrim Mothers. I was drawn instantly to her warm, bubbly and enthusiastic nature as we chatted away easily on all sorts of topics.

In mid-January 2011, I decided to spend a long weekend in Pilgrim Country – an area with a radius of about thirty miles, covering parts of Nottinghamshire, Lincolnshire, South Yorkshire and Leicestershire towards the East of England, where the Pilgrims' leaders originated. It is an aspirational tourist area that is not well known, even locally, as the Pilgrims barely get a mention in the UK. Visiting there is a pilgrimage for Americans rather than for Brits. I suppose there's been a lot of history since a small group of Pilgrim families waved goodbye nearly four centuries ago. So it's up to a small number of dedicated locals to keep the history alive.

I had had some phone conversations with one of them, Anthony Darbyshire, who is Chair of the Pilgrim Fathers UK Origins Association. He had kindly offered me space outside his farmhouse to park my motorhome on the Friday evening. As it was a typical dreary January day, a short journey time was more important than scenery, so, my dogs and I made our way, from Kenilworth, along mainly motorways and dual carriageways in peak Friday afternoon traffic.

I spent an evening that was by contrast far from dreary, chatting about the Pilgrims with Anthony in the lounge of his home, sharing the sofa with his friendly dog. On the Saturday morning we collected Jane Williams from Retford Station. Jane is an award-winning Producer/Director who specialises in factual programmes. We had struck up a friendship and working relationship over our mutual love of stories.

Jane was coming to take some still shots and video footage of the Pilgrim Country and its stories. She was easy to spot as she walked along the platform in her usual bright colours – a red coat on this occasion – and her dark, flowing hair with its hint of a wave. I felt rather scruffy in my blue waterproof jacket, thick woollen sweater and denim jeans complete with walking boots; but I suppose my focus had been on warmth and practicality with spending a few days in the motorhome during the depths of a severe winter.

Anthony took us first to Babworth Church where the Pilgrims had gathered to be inspired and entranced by the stirring words of Richard Clyfton, Rector of Babworth Church from 1555 to 1605. Families would travel sometimes as far as twelve miles to join this congregation. Many of them would walk the Great North Road, which runs alongside the church. It sounds grand, but it's actually a muddy track. So, it puts into perspective just some of the dedication needed by families to attend this church. For most people, however, this would have been their week's highlight.

After picking up Julie Dunstan in the car park of The Pilgrim Fathers pub in Scrooby, we set off to meet Sue at Gainsborough Old Hall, about a twenty-five minute drive away. When I had set off, I had not really thought about the parking. So when we turned into quite a small but busy public car park near the Old Hall, I said a little prayer that I'd get in and out safely. I'd had the van a little over a month and I was still getting used to its size. Thankfully, there were two parking bays in the middle I could straddle front and rear. I breathed in deeply, willing the van to contract in size as I successfully negotiated the space. Phew!

The Hall is a large black and white half-timbered building with a grassed area in front – a typical English building, full of character. We walked through the entrance and down a few steps into a cosy shop area with warm lighting and shelves full of various souvenirs and guidebooks. Given pride of place was a freestanding display holding dozens of Sue's book, *Tudor Rose*. A few minutes later, the writer herself appeared with a beaming smile on her face. We hugged like old friends.

Sue welcomed us into the Hall and took Jane and me on our private tour. Sue has a stunning ability to bring places to life. She engages her audience with her expressive voice and mannerisms. When we stopped at the portrait of Lady Rose Hickman, the Tudor Rose displayed on the book cover downstairs, Sue was positively electrifying. Totally mesmerised, we entered into Sue's world where she mixed her own story with that of Rose, which you can participate in later too. When we re-joined Julie for tea and cakes in the bright, high-ceilinged café with the large screen doors pulled across, it seemed worlds and centuries away from the room of Rose's portrait upstairs.

After this occasion I was to meet Sue several times at Scrooby Manor as Julie, Jane, Sue and I deepened our friendship, maybe just like those original Pilgrim Mothers…

Today, Sue and I sit in the music room of Scrooby Manor, home to much of the Pilgrims' history in England, at the invitation of the 'Lady of the Manor', Julie. So, welcome to Sue Allan's world, where fact combines with fiction in such a way that it all seems at the same time real yet unbelievable.

Sue, you have written amazing stories about some incredible women in the past. But you've got a pretty amazing story yourself. Tell me about it.

Well, I had a very difficult beginning. I had a mother who shouldn't have had children, so life was pretty difficult for me. I suffered a number of incidents with her, starting with when I was just six months old and she poured a saucepan of boiling water over me as I sat in a highchair. I was lucky to survive that. Growing up, I just suffered abuse from her until the age of fifteen when I ran away. I couldn't tell anybody what was going on when I was young. I didn't speak till late. And then when speech came, it was so slurred and such a problem I had to have speech therapy for five or six years, and that was very isolating. So, no, not a very good beginning.

I would say it affected my confidence in life. If you had told me that now, in my fifties, I'd be out talking to audiences, sometimes of about 100 people, I wouldn't have believed you. And as for writing the books, no, I wouldn't have had the confidence. So, yes, my life is not how I expected it to be, and to find the subjects that I've written about has been life-changing.

So, tell me what you write about.

I write about the Pilgrim connection to Gainsborough Old Hall, but it began in a very strange way. I was approaching fifty. I was not in a very good place. My husband had left me. I was left with two teenagers to finish bringing up, and my youngest, Laurence, was autistic. So, it's not as if there was going to be any great career opening for me. I'd been a stay-at-home mother for twenty years and I thought that was my life set. I was just going to be my son's carer – we were on benefits. Not a very good outlook. Very bleak.

And then one afternoon, I had some time to myself. I'd not been in Lincolnshire very long before my husband had left me and I went to this manor house called Gainsborough Old Hall. I found myself standing in one of the chambers, looking up at the portrait of a seventy-year-old woman, all dressed in black, with what some say is quite a severe face. The portrait was inscribed 'Rose, Daughter of Sir William Locke. Married to Anthony Hickman.' It was also conveniently dated 1596. I immediately became mesmerised by her and wondered about her life. And though I didn't know it at the time, that was a moment that completely changed my life around.

Nobody could tell me anything more about her, other than she lived at the Old Hall and she probably sheltered the Pilgrim Fathers in her house, which I thought was quite daring. Straight away, I thought, *Wow, this is a feisty lady*. It piqued my curiosity, but it would be another five or six years before I found out who she was – Lady Rose Hickman – and her story. In that time, I'd made my own journey, which had entwined with hers in such an amazing way that I couldn't have made it up!

Not knowing about her but knowing she had hidden the Pilgrim Fathers, I thought, *Right, I want to find out more about that connection.* And in the end, that led me to writing a book when I was pushing fifty. I mean, who did I think I was to write a novel? I had written a *poem* before; I won a WI poetry competition. And that was the limit of my writing since I'd left school. Yet I wrote that book, and throughout writing it, I would wake up at night and hear Lady Rose Hickman, the lady in that portrait, talking to me. It was at that point where I thought I was losing the plot. Well, for an author ... that's not good! *[Laughter]* But I really did begin to doubt my sanity. I thought that with the pressure of

> "I would wake up at night and hear Lady Rose Hickman, the lady in that portrait, talking to me. It was at that point where I thought I was losing the plot. Well, for an author ... that's not good!"

my life, living on virtually nothing, a deserted wife writing a book, maybe I was going to have a breakdown. I mean, hearing a dead woman talking to you in the middle of the night … it's not only odd, it's quite frightening.

I started to realise the things she told me were actually true and, through that connection with her, the first book I did write was about a maidservant, actually a maidservant of Rose Hickman. And it started the whole ball rolling to where I am now. As I was researching that and the Pilgrim Fathers' history, I was picking up skills. I was absorbing the history, and in such a way that not only could I write a novel, but I could also go out and talk to people about the subject. I could stand in front of a small audience and then a bigger audience and then bigger still. And soon I'd have people coming to me to ask my opinion. And then, I could actually do my own research on the Pilgrims.

It became so absorbing, but all the time I had this Rose Hickman in the back of my mind, and I didn't know that I was travelling towards her and finding her story. It was just incredible.

So what was it that started you writing your first book, *Mayflower Maid*?

Well, the reason I started writing, and it sounds absolutely ludicrous *[laughing]*, was I'd got this connection with Rose and that portrait, and at the same time I really fell in love with Gainsborough Old Hall and everything about it. So I kept going back and reading whatever I could find about the place. I would come back and gaze at Rose's portrait again and again. And blow me, at the end of that first year, just a few months after I'd seen her, the position of Keeper of Gainsborough Old Hall came up and Lincolnshire Council advertised the position.

Now, I'm naïve because, as it was advertised in the newspaper, I thought, *Right, I can apply for that.* I didn't know they'd already chosen somebody in-house but at that point they had to advertise outside to be legally compliant. So although I applied, there wasn't really any realistic chance that I was going to get the job. I didn't know that, so I went for it, and I went for it in a big way. I produced plans of how they could increase visitor numbers … everything. I went the whole hog. It didn't matter to me that I hadn't worked for so many years; but it obviously mattered to the people who interviewed me.

> "… as I left the room … I turned around and … heard someone talking … I realised, to my horror, it was 'me' … saying to them, ' … I'll go away and write a book, set here.'"

I could see, as the interview went on, they were stony-faced. There was no interaction with me and I was thinking, *I can't read them*, and I find it hard to read people's faces anyway. So I thought, *Right, I've given it my best shot*, and we shook hands. Then as I left the room, I don't know why, but I turned around and … heard someone talking … And then I realised, to my horror, it was *me* talking, and I was saying to them, "Right, if you don't give me the position, that's fine. Use all the information I've given you, all my ideas with my blessing, and in the meantime I'll go away and write a book, set here."

I couldn't believe I'd said that. I don't know where it came from. I'm sure, as I shut that door, I could hear them laughing. I don't know whether that just spurred me on all the more, but I went away and started on that book. I was going to do it. There were no two ways about it. I'd said I was going to do it and somehow, I don't know how, but I did it. It took me nine months to research and write that book. Just nine months, and I never looked back.

The perfect gestation period for the birth of your first baby!

Yes, though finding a publisher was difficult. But then finally I got word from one. "We're going to publish your book." It was Christmas Eve. It couldn't have been a better Christmas present. *Mayflower Maid* was actually published the following year in July 2005, a few weeks after my fiftieth birthday. It was just amazing.

And then, by the September of the same year, I was standing in New England, in Plymouth, Massachusetts, giving a talk at the invitation of some descendants of the real life Pilgrim Fathers that appeared in that first book. It was just incredible.

Now, when you say 'Pilgrim Fathers', do you mean the fathers or the families?

I mean the families, but I say the Pilgrim Fathers because although the story – and my particular book, *Mayflower Maid* – was about a Pilgrim woman, the Pilgrim women are never really considered. It's always the Pilgrim Fathers, mainly because we don't know about many of the Pilgrim Mothers' lives. We know their names in places. The character in my novel *Mayflower Maid* was based on a real life maidservant, but we know nothing about her in reality. I fictionalised her life and led her through the story because women just weren't even thought of. It was a man's world. And this particular woman, I didn't even know her name. I had to research to find it because on the *Mayflower* Ship Manifest, she's just listed as a maidservant to John Carver. They hadn't even bothered to give the poor woman her name, which is awful. To come into life and then disappear out again with nobody even bothering to record your name … yet you're in the middle of this great story. It just shows how women tend to get treated; very much then as an afterthought and, I'm afraid, sometimes today as an afterthought. So I gave this woman back an identity; that was satisfying.

> "To come into life and then disappear out again with nobody even bothering to record your name … yet you're in the middle of this great story."

So, although the story I've written is fictionalised in parts, at least she's now got a name and a life to be remembered for. In fact, I could only find her name because William Bradford, the Governor of Plymouth, wrote down at the back of his Plymouth Plantation journal all the original settlers who had died and had children. In addition, in 1623 there was record of a division of cattle where everyone was named. (Men *and* women were entitled to a division of land and cattle.) So, by matching the names of everybody who'd arrived on the *Mayflower* and died with everybody who was given these cattle, I could work out there was a Mr Eaton who had a wife called Dorothy. They'd married in the New World, so she must have come on the *Mayflower*. Yet she's the only one not given a name on the manifest. I knew Dorothy had to be the maidservant. But how awful that you have to research to give her her name back when she suffered all the hardships that the men suffered. All the deprivation. And to be forgotten. It seems so unfair.

What do we know about the women, the Pilgrim Mothers?

Well, their challenges began in England even before that journey to the New World. They had to escape the authorities, and that's no mean feat. It's okay for a bunch of men to have their principles and go off on some adventure. But the women had no option. They were the homemakers, the mothers, and where the men went, they had to go. And that meant the children as well.

So, even back in England, when our group had to escape, the women were tagging along with the children. That must have been so hard. It's one thing to put yourself at peril, but tending to your children too? Take Mary Brewster, William Brewster's wife, who lived here at Scrooby Manor. Look what she had to give up. When they made the escape from England, she'd not long had a baby. She had young children and a babe in arms when they were on the run between Scrooby and Boston, hiding, travelling all the back roads, not lighting fires at night. It's a sixty-mile journey. It must have taken them at least six days. Can you imagine going out with a baby? No hot food, nowhere to wash a diaper or linen. How do you keep them warm when it's autumn and you're sleeping out? It must have been horrendous, and it's the women who bore the brunt of this. They were following their men. They were supporting their men and their children and that must have been hard.

You can't help, as a woman, but feel for those women. Men will probably not even think about it. It's just the background story to the men's adventure, not very glamorous, and oh so easily forgotten in history. I think that's why I feel great empathy for them and other women who are passed by.

> "You can't help, as a woman, but feel for those women. ... oh so easily forgotten in history. I think that's why I feel great empathy for them and other women who are passed by."

They were fleeing religious persecution, weren't they? They wanted to practise their religion in their own way. Free speech.

It's all about those simple liberties. We take them for granted, but other people have to suffer for them, and the women suffered the most. The men couldn't have done any of it without the women behind them, and yet they're the ones that don't get the mention. It's like a ghostwriter of a book. Someone else gets all the glory and the person who did the real work is forgotten. It's so unfair.

About Mary Brewster – you were talking about her and her family having to get to Boston. Was that the first attempt to escape to the Netherlands?

That's right. And that ended in utter humiliation because they were thwarted at Boston. They'd hired a ship to take them across to Holland and the captain and his crew had betrayed them. That must have been awful for the women in particular because the men were rounded up and herded off, and the women were searched beforehand. They were physically searched by these rough sailors going in amongst their clothing.

In those days, if you had valuables, you would keep them in your pockets. The pockets were actually pockets tied on a string around a woman's waist, under her undergarments. And we didn't have underwear as such; we had petticoats. So can you imagine these rough sailors daring to go amongst your undergarments? How humiliating.

And then you can imagine the children crying and the men being herded off, taken to prison. They were held in Boston in the Guild Hall, but the women weren't important enough to be imprisoned because they were considered as chattels. They were their husband's belongings with no mind of their own, so they were just left on the street to fend for themselves, for weeks on end. I mean, that really must have brought the message home to them about just how worthless they were in the eyes of society, that they weren't even worthy of locking up. At least they would have been fed if they'd been locked up. Instead, they were on the street with children.

> "They were their husband's belongings ... [chattels] ... so they were just left on the street to fend for themselves, for weeks on end."

How awful. It's incredible that you have so little standing socially that you're not even worthy of prison.

And so what happened after that first failed attempt?

Well, eventually, the men were released and the whole group hid out over the winter months before they could make a second attempt the following spring. And in that time, the women fared even worse because the second attempt almost ended in failure. At that point, the men did get away from the Humber, but the women by a misfortune had been stranded on a barge on the shore. The tide had turned and when the main ship came, they couldn't get out to it. By the time they were trying to get themselves together, the searchers, obviously looking for the men, came across the women. The men scarpered and the women were sitting ducks.

Again, they were rounded up but they had no use, no worth. They weren't worth any collateral. They were just a burden. They were bundled up and nobody really knew what to do with them, so they were taken from place to place. If you were taken to a town and held, the townspeople would have to pay for your upkeep. And of course, you don't want to pay for a bunch of women and brats. They got moved on and eventually released because they were just women. They weren't the instigators. They weren't going to be held accountable for what the men were doing because they had no importance. It's not as if they had made the decision for themselves because women weren't capable of making decisions for themselves.

And how did they eventually escape? Is that recorded at all?

William Bradford does write that by one way or another they were spirited away. We think that the men came back, like little raiding parties, and managed to round up the women one by one and get them across to Holland. So, they were rescued and taken over and eventually did meet with their menfolk and the children. But that must have been an awful time, when they were left behind. How do you support yourself if your man is gone and he's your breadwinner, and you've sold off everything you've got? Who cares for you? Who protects you? How do you make your way in that sort of society? Here, today, a lone woman has help. At least we can go places and get bread on the table for the children. In those days, it must have been frightening. And where were these men? Were they going to come back for you? Did they get away safely? Are they dead?

And they did go over to the Netherlands because there was a community that had been established over there, wasn't there? Of the same religious persuasion.

There were other refugees, yes, in Amsterdam. And then after a year, our Scrooby group moved on to Leiden; but their life would have been so different to the life here. For one, at that time in England, we were very much connected to the land. By going to Holland, we wouldn't have been. Land was very scarce so they were living in cities which would have been quite strange. A completely alien way of life.

And also there's the other thing. How do you support yourself? You're taking whatever jobs you can and the jobs that are going to be open to you aren't going to be la crème de la crème because you're a foreign refugee. You're at the bottom of the pile. It's a struggle. Even if there are other people like you, your fellow countrymen over there are all in the same boat. You're outsiders in a foreign country. Again, that's difficult.

Imagine going to a market, trying to buy food, and you don't speak the language. It must have been hard, but the women survived that. They survived it for some twelve years, and maybe some of them had got settled, thinking, *We've raised our children here. We're getting used to the life*, and then suddenly, 1620, the men are moving on. They can't go back to England; they're finding it uncomfortable in Holland … "I know, we'll all go to the New World," and the New World at that time was a jolly place. We had the colony at Virginia and the life expectancy was not very good. By 1620, they'd already pumped in over 8,000 colonists, but they still couldn't get the number of live colonists to stay above the 1,000 mark. So, not very promising. "Come here and die" should have been the motto.

So the women were on their way to that. I don't know what my point of view would have been at that time, to be faced with that. What a prospect. We're going to a New World where we might not live that long. More hardship, more starting over, but in an even harsher environment. No family. No grandmas with you or aunts or extended support.

They must have been terrified, but they went. A lot of them died, but those who survived the first winter then had to face more deprivation the following year and almost starvation conditions at times. That's a lot to ask from a wife, isn't it? Then all that sacrifice not noted. It's criminal really, when you look at it. *[Laughing ironically]* I know I'm laughing, but if that had been me … to think all I struggled for would be forgotten and only the men would be remembered…

But it's through women like you, telling the stories so that they can be remembered, and they can be celebrated and recognised again. They certainly need to be.

They do, but the shame is this was 400 years ago. It's taken 400 years to get into the position where women can do that. It just seems so wrong. It's been so long a wait, but it's not too late, and I think it's right that we remember women in the past like the Pilgrim Mothers, such as Rose Hickman's story. An amazing story, and yet nobody had looked at her life fully until I'd stood before that picture and wondered who she was and then began to piece it together. This is another woman from the Tudor era, a woman who wrote an account of much of her life, which seems to have just been smoothed over and forgotten.

So tell me her story, Sue.

Her story is incredible. She was born in London to a very wealthy family. Her father was Henry VIII's royal mercer and very close to Henry.[2] He had a key to his bedroom. Anything the royal household wanted, he procured. But he had an interesting sideline. While England was still Catholic, he was smuggling in Tyndale's English Bibles, which meant if he'd been caught, he would have been burnt as a heretic. And Rose writes that not only was her father doing this – and one of his clients was Anne Boleyn no less – but her mother was reading to her and her younger sister, as children, in her mother's chamber. And Rose writes that her mother read from these same good books but only in private for fear of trouble.

I love it! Rose says, "…for fear of trouble", not for fear of execution. Trouble. And Rose would have known trouble because another Bible smuggler, known to the family, was actually shot dead outside Rose's house in Cheapside for doing what her father was doing. So the danger was very real, but Rose dismisses it as trouble.

And she writes about what it was like during the Reformation when England became Catholic. Rose was a young mother by then and had to escape from her own country for her religious beliefs, as did her husband and many other members of her family. And that's amazing. But she had also helped others out of the country before then, with her husband, and that suffering must have stayed with Rose. Living through that persecution, taking her children, being on the run, being an exile, must have meant she resonated well with a group of Separatists that turned up at Gainsborough, when she was an old woman of eighty, who were going through very much the same thing as she had when she was young.

It's your life playing out. These people were fighting for the same sort of religious freedoms that her father, her mother, her siblings had fought for, and her own children, and they still hadn't achieved them. But the fight was still on. And she was game. She was going to help them. You just can't help but admire that sort of spirit, can you? This defiance, if you like. An amazing woman.

And did you find some connection with Rose? Is my memory correct? Do you come from London originally?

I come from London and the connection, when it came out, actually threw me because this is some five years on from when I first saw her portrait. I'd written two more books after *Mayflower Maid* and they became a New World trilogy. The story of the maidservant carried on. And I found myself, in the very last chapter of my third book *Restoration Lady,* taking the story away from Lincolnshire and back to where I grew up in Merton.

I didn't have a very good childhood, as I told you, and when I was young, something awful happened. My brother, who was nineteen, bless him, died. He had Hodgkin's disease and back then you couldn't cure it. The sad situation for me was that I was already having an unbearable time at home, but when my brother died, I couldn't even talk about him at home. I wasn't even allowed to attend his funeral, so trying to come to terms with his death was awful. I couldn't do that within the home. My mother made that impossible. But I did find sanctuary in a church in Merton called St Mary's the Virgin, and that became my haunt. I never attended that church because my mother

---

2   A mercer was a trader, especially in fine fabrics.

wouldn't allow me to. But churches weren't locked in those days, so there was nothing to stop me – I was eleven – from wandering in and sitting down and crying and grieving. And that's what I did.

Once I'd told the vicar why I was there, he never said, "Little girl, get out of here." If I was there and I wanted to say hello or wanted to talk, I could talk. If I didn't, they knew I was there and they left me alone. And I had my own little spot in the chancel, next to the organ. So, sometimes the organist would be there and I could hear him, and that was where I went to try to make some sense of my life.

When I'd written that church into my third book, I actually wrote to St Mary's the Virgin to tell them what I'd done, because by this time I had people turning up to Gainsborough Old Hall who'd read *Mayflower Maid*. It was brilliant having people come there because they'd read my words. So out of courtesy, I wrote to the church and told them they were going to be in this book, and very shortly after, I received a brown envelope and it had a guidebook in it.

The guidebook said that in 1536 the plague in London was very, very bad and a family moved from London to Merton (which was seven miles outside London at that time – it's now a part of London) to escape the plague. They took a house by the church. And the following year, 1537, the plague was even worse, so the family went back and became benefactors of the church there. But sadly, in the October, when the daughter of the family was eleven, the same age as I was, Mrs Locke died. She died in childbirth and was buried in the church.

> "Something happens in life and you don't know it's a turning point. And my life turned at that point, out of all recognition."

Locke! I remembered that name, Locke, because Rose's portrait has 'Rose. Daughter of Sir William Locke' written on it. Locke's a common name, but as I read on in the guidebook, it said that later in life the daughter of the family, Rose, wrote an account of her life and how she and her husband, Anthony, had helped wanted Protestants out of the country in the reign of Queen Mary. I knew then, in a second, that was my Rose. So, when I was eleven, my brother had died in the October and I'd gone to that church to grieve. When Rose was eleven, her mother had died in the October and was buried in that church.

There's no memorial there to mark the spot today, but when I got hold of the historian who had researched the guidebook – because none of this was known when I was a child – and I told him my story, he then explained to me that actually, through his own research, he found out that Rose's mother had been buried round about where I used to sit in the chancel, next to the organ. So when I was eleven, grieving, Rose's mother was under my feet.

Wow, Sue! That is amazing. The connection was already there. Did you find the connection continuing as you got older?

Well, I left Merton when I was fifteen. I ran away from home, and I never went back until last year. All those decades, I never went back. And yet through a fluke, I moved up here to Lincolnshire. My family moved here – my husband and children. A house we wanted to buy in the south, in the West Country, in Devon, had fallen through. We came up here on a visit, saw the house I live in now and bought it. I was never meant to come all this way to Lincolnshire. I didn't even know Lincolnshire existed, and then I'm stood before this portrait of this woman, wondering who she was.

It was just incredible. Something happens in life and you don't know it's a turning point. And my life turned at that point, out of all recognition. Looking back, it's as if I was meant to be there. I was meant to come face to face with her, wonder who she was, hear about the pilgrims, write about them, become involved with them and then, through writing these three books, discover that she came from Merton. And then, through that lucky link with that historian in Merton, I found Rose's writings that had been presumed lost. At last, I could have her own words in her own handwriting, in front of me. I had Rose. It was like she was sitting where you are, talking to me. "Come on Sue, this is what you want to know. This is my life." It's something that is so incredible.

Do you have any explanation, any thoughts?

[Shaking her head] Other than I was meant to do it. I was meant to write about her. I was meant to find her story and to bring it alive. I'm meant to bring the story of those Pilgrim Mothers alive at this particular time. I don't know why now, but I very much suspect that when I look back in another ten years' time, perhaps it's going to come clear.

But with the links I've found with Rose that have led me onto other links, like here to Scrooby, it seems impossible for me to believe that this is all down to chance. Chance doesn't throw up the coincidences that have been thrown up in my journey. This is a journey that I was meant to make, but I wasn't meant to make it alone. I was meant to start on this journey and meet other people to join me on it, and I have. And we're all going along this road together now and it's a lovely feeling. A very satisfying feeling because in our wake, we're actually churning up history, identities, giving something back to lost people, even if it's just their name and what they did. And that's very, very rewarding. I can't explain that feeling. It's just wonderful, and as I say, it's changed my life. And I'm sure it will keep on changing me. I don't know where this journey is going, but I'm not frightened and I'm not alone. Let's carry on down the road.

> "I was meant to find her story and to bring it alive. I'm meant to bring the story of those Pilgrim Mothers alive at this particular time."

What about the future?

I don't know where the future's going. I don't know where this is going. And to be honest that's the least of my worries. I'm just enjoying the journey. I don't know. I'm not forcing it in any direction. No, I'm a happy passenger. I'm being led, and I'm very happy to just go with it. Because if it's anything like the last five or six years, it's going to be really interesting, and I'm going to meet wonderful people along the way. So, I've got no fears. I've got no worries. Bring it on.

Fantastic, Sue. Is there anything more you'd like to add?

The one thing I would like to say is I wish somebody could have said to me when I was in that really dark place, when I started to write or even wondering whether I should even apply for that job, "The only person holding you back is yourself." That would have helped.

And the other thing is you need luck, and if only someone had explained to me that luck is preparation meeting opportunity, I could have driven forward a lot more confidently. They're the two things that I have learnt. Never say never. You're the one that's holding you back from getting where you need to go. Only you. And if you can just have the courage to throw off that leash and not hold yourself back, who knows where you're going to end up? I didn't.

That's brilliant. The only other thing I wanted to ask you is about your autistic son. Was it tough as a single parent dealing with that?

"Luck is preparation meeting opportunity."

No, it wasn't tough because we had Laurence diagnosed from about the time he went to playschool, when he was about four. By going through that process and speaking with the professionals dealing with him, with lots of questions they ask you, it soon started to become clear that I also have autism. When I saw the attitude towards Laurence in professionals' eyes change and when I would have someone talking to me saying, "Of course, children like these…" I began to fully appreciate the stigma that's attached to that diagnosis. So when I was offered the chance to go through the full diagnosis myself after he had been labelled as autistic, I decided to get my diagnosis abroad … so I wouldn't have to face the stigma. I'd always known there was something different about me from when I was young, and I couldn't understand why I felt like an alien, even as a child. So, I have that bond with my son.

I have Asperger's Syndrome – high functioning autism. So, without that label, I think I got further than I would have done, not being diagnosed until my late forties. So I want more for him and I don't see this as something to be ashamed of. I don't think we would have come out of our caves if there hadn't been the odd person who was different. And we do see the world differently. I see the world differently. Maybe that's why I'm good at research and other things. People say to me, "How do you work that out? How do you join certain things together in your research?" I've got that sort of mind and I think it's my autism. So, no, I won't hide it and I won't apologise for him.

I've come to the point in the last few years where, actually, I won't apologise for myself having Asperger's either. Why should I? I'm not ashamed of it, and I don't think anyone should be. We're just wired differently. So, no, I don't hide that away from my son. We have a very good bond, and because I see him going through things that I might have gone through when I was younger, I can help him. But yes, that was a clear decision of mine. I would not have my diagnosis in England. I do not want to be sixty … what am I saying? I'm nearly sixty now ... I don't want to be seventy or eighty and have a stroke or something, and if attitudes are as they are now, the first thing people read in my notes is 'Has/had Asperger's Syndrome' or autism – because it would change their perception of me. So, I'm going rogue at the moment.

"You laugh at us because we're different. We laugh at you because you're all the same."

One of the things they always throw in with autism and Asperger's is this 'no imagination'. My son has a wonderful imagination for stories. And for me, people say, "How can you bring history alive? You have a wonderful imagination." I've been outside today researching Scrooby Manor. It's not here anymore, just a tiny part; but I know what was in that place. I understand how it was built.

I have a similar experience with Gainsborough Old Hall. I have an inventory of what it was like in 1625, about the time that *Mayflower Maid* was set in. I reconstruct that building in my head from the information I have. I use the information, so I don't imagine it. I see it, and I see it in 3D. 'Normal' people don't do that. So yes, we do things that are a bit quirky. But if you were to ask me if I would like to be different or if I would like Laurence's autism taken away, no, because it makes us different. Laurence has a t-shirt that he loves and I think it sums it up. It says quite simply, 'You laugh at us because we're different. We laugh at you because you're all the same.' *[Laughter]* I think I'd like that on my gravestone.

What a wonderful epitaph! I think a few people might want to use that one!

Sue's story for me demonstrates the old adage that truth is stranger than fiction at times. Such synchronicities led to her story intertwining with that of Rose and the other Pilgrim Mothers. And as Sue says, it's often not till you look back that you can see how everything was meant to be and has led to your life's magical journey.

I too found that once I knew my mission, rather like Sue discovering Rose (though maybe Rose was always with her), life took on a different focus. That's not to say it didn't still take me a while to get to the point of writing about modern Pilgrim Mothers. However, when I look back on the last few years, I can see how everything has fitted together perfectly. Although I was anxious to progress and impatient to reach my first stage destination, despite not being sure exactly what that was, I can see how certain delays were needed in order for me to learn necessary skills, digest important lessons and connect with specific women – and much more.

Yet what I also know is that only I can facilitate the birth of this book. This is my story and it's time to tell it along with those of other women's. Like Sue, my story is intertwined with the stories of the other women in this book, and in reality with all women. There's something that women understand without words. Maybe it's our biology, our hard wiring, our personal history; I'm not sure. All I know is that the women I meet now are very much an integral part of my journey. And as Sue rightly says, you gather others along the way, each on our path, and it's exhilarating and heartening to recognise we're all combining at this special time in history.

I love J.R.R. Tolkien's quote, 'Not all those who wander are lost'. At times I've felt lost, but I've carried on till I've been able to reach a way-stage and look back and clearly see the path. I see how my passion for people, stories and travelling has combined at the age of sixty into this miraculous tapestry that's unfolding right now.

When I'm with Sue, I feel infected with her sense of wonder about how her life's turned out and her wide-eyed enthusiasm for her subjects. Anyone who joins one of Sue's guided tours doesn't just get a story; they get a full-blown pilgrimage experience of what it was like to be those people and suffer the hardships, along with the wonderment of how strong human courage can be.

Sue may be, and indeed is, a modern Pilgrim Mother, but she's very much rooted in bringing the past into the present so that these stories, hidden for hundreds of years, continue to breathe life and inspiration into future generations. Long may her stories, and those of other amazing women, be told.

"The women I meet now are very much an integral part of my journey."

JANE NOBLE KNIGHT

JULIE DUNSTAN

" We take all waifs and strays and, as the sign in the kitchen says, 'Come in as strangers, leave as friends.' "

Julie Dunstan lives with her husband, David, her mother, Joyce, daughter, Kamila, and two dogs in David's childhood home – Scrooby Manor in Nottinghamshire, UK. Scrooby Manor was home to William and Mary Brewster, Pilgrims who sailed to America on the *Mayflower* in 1620. Julie has spent over thirty years in a nursing career, latterly in the field of pain management. The rest of her time is spent working in the community supporting village life, adding to the knowledge of the Pilgrim families and volunteering for the Jumbulance Trust.

www.pilgrimfathersorigins.org/Pilgrim_Fathers_Origins_Tour_Scrooby_Manor.html

A Conversation With
Julie Dunstan

Lady of Scrooby Manor

Have you ever woken up and known with total clarity that you needed to make your way to a certain place? Today was to be just such a day for me. It was 7.30 am on a cold Saturday November morning in 2010. A severe winter had already begun. Curtains still drawn, I awoke in the front bedroom of my parents' large semi-detached house in a suburb of Preston, Lancashire, where they had lived for over fifty years. That state of repose lasted mere seconds.

I had moved back in with my parents about two weeks previously, having been given notice to quit on the house I had rented for a year in Newport, Shropshire. My life seemed to have been in transition for several years. Maybe that's just the lot of a pilgrim. It was as if I wasn't meant to be settling anywhere for the time being.

With two dogs there were few places available to rent. Around the same time, my parents' cleaner/helper had broken her ankle, so they invited me to stay with them temporarily and help out. I stored my furniture and boxes in their double garage and squeezed my dogs and myself into the house.

Over six months earlier, Sandy Edwards of The Healing Trust had asked me to run a one-hour workshop for carers and therapists as part of a Retreat Day at Studley Castle, near Redditch in Warwickshire. Sandy had always impressed me with her dedication, energy and enthusiasm, so I agreed without hesitation.

We had first met in 2007 when Sandy was looking for a workshop facilitator at short notice. I received her SOS via a friend's friend in Dubai. (Some emails take the scenic route.) I duly delivered what would be the first of several workshops for Sandy and so started our relationship.

The problem with the Retreat Day, however, was that I was now living 150 miles away, three times the distance. The weather through the week had been deteriorating, so the evening before I had virtually talked myself into not going. However, something stopped me actually making the phone call.

So there I was that morning just 'knowing' I had to make the journey. Packing my dogs into the car I set off through freezing fog, snow and ice, hazard lights on the motorway … the works. I had no chance of making the ten o'clock greeting and meditation, but I reckoned I could make the first session at eleven o'clock. I left a message for Sandy with the hotel to that effect and did indeed make it in time – by the skin of my teeth.

I went straight into my workshop on 'Finding Your Life's Purpose' and mentioned my own 'Pilgrim Mother' mission. I repeated the workshop in the afternoon as another facilitator had cancelled.

At the end, a woman who introduced herself as Gillian came up to me and said, "My niece Julie Dunstan lives in one of the original Pilgrims' houses. It's called Scrooby Manor. I'm speaking to her this next week. Would you like me to introduce you?"

Aha, I thought to myself. *So that's why I had to be here today.* On waking I had felt that sense of anticipation I always feel before meeting someone who is to be significant. When I met Gillian, I actually didn't know how special Scrooby Manor was, being the home of William and Mary Brewster, but I was soon to find out.

A few days later, I phoned Julie and arranged my first of several visits to her home.

Julie had a friendly, gentle, unassuming voice, not a bit as I had expected for someone living in a 'Manor'. However, as she says in the following conversation, it's not quite as you may imagine it to be…

I join Julie and her husband David, and Sue Allan (Second chapter) and her husband Roger in the music room of Scrooby Manor, near Retford in Nottinghamshire. I am arriving slightly later than planned so they have finished the beautiful lunch Julie had prepared of light bites followed by scones with jam, cream and strawberries. Fortunately, there is plenty left for me too! I feel a sense of history repeating itself as many Pilgrim Families would have met in this very room with their hosts, the Brewsters. I wonder if their gatherings were always as relaxed as today's, chatting, giving updates and talking about future plans. I was sure not, given the religious persecution which led them to leave their home suddenly and escape to the Netherlands – eventually.

Today, after half an hour's catch up with everyone, Julie and I are left to chat, as she shares the story of her life and how Scrooby Manor came to be her home.

Tell me about your life growing up and how you came to be living here, Julie.

I actually come from Henley-in-Arden, so Shakespeare country. And we moved up north with my dad's work. I went to school nearby in Retford, where I met David, my husband. We were friends all through high school. We did attempt going out twice and then on the third time, we actually got it together. So after that we finally married and I then moved into Scrooby. I was about twenty-four. His family business was comprised of two farms. They were dairy, arable and beef farmers. His father was totally in control, as farming fathers usually are. There were two brothers; the daughters didn't want anything to do with the farm.

I'd always loved Scrooby Manor but didn't see any way we'd ever live here, as it was David's brother's home. We lived in the other farm then. We'd converted the cottage into a modern living space because that was a bit of a relic too, like the Manor. And that's where we both found we had a flair for doing up older properties.

David worked on the farm for about the first fifteen years of our marriage, but we felt very restricted. He felt very much held down and I've always been a free spirit, like all my family. They'd always encouraged me and been very positive. That rubbed off on David, which caused quite a few family problems because he always wanted to develop things or branch out and expand the business, but it was a closed shop. So, it was very hard.

"I've always been a free spirit, like all my family. They'd always encouraged me and been very positive."

Nevertheless, we ended up buying a property, doing it up and renting it out … and then another. We also had a butcher shop, for the farm animals, so we knew where the meat had come from, and a delicatessen opposite where we did cooked meats and various concoctions of sausages and other specialities. So, we gathered a bit of business sense between us.

At the end of the village, there was this house we kept walking past and dreaming about. One day, thinking we'd never be able to afford it, I said, "If we ever got this house, I'd run round naked on the lawn with a lit candle shoved where it shouldn't be, singing *Yankee Doodle Dandy*." Anyway, two years later, we bought it. The owner had found out we were interested and he wanted us to have it – just like that. He knocked the price down for us and that was it. So we were on the property ladder again.

And did you fulfil your… ?

[Laughing] I did, with a friend, under the cover of darkness and with David not allowed outside. But I knew he hid in the bushes because I was aware of them shaking because he was laughing. So I did indeed keep my word.

But, you know, we still weren't really satisfied. We wanted to do things and grow. So we went on holiday to New Zealand to see a friend who'd emigrated. We fell in love with the place, both of us separately, but we didn't say anything to each other. Then when we got home, we were unsettled. In the end, it came out that we would both love to live there, but David said, "No, I daren't."

So I said, "Okay. We'll put it on the backburner and look at it for the future."

Then of course farming went downhill and so did the profits from milk. Supermarkets were getting the monopoly. There was Foot and Mouth Disease and Creutzfeldt-Jakob disease (CJD) – the human form of BSE (mad cow disease) – and all the new regulations coming in. So David's family ended up selling the farming business. That was quite sad because it was the end of an era. We had more than 200 cows that weren't selling, so we had to put them all down. That was hard. The way of life changed and a lot of the land was sold off.

But at the same time it was our opportunity to go abroad. So, we took another holiday in New Zealand and saw a place we liked. We actually attended the auction on holiday. We've never done anything like that before – just on a whim. We sat there, and at the end the auctioneer came over and asked, "Are you interested?"

We hesitated. "Well, tentatively, yes."

At that point, we had no residency visas or anything like that. However, we went into negotiations and were told to put a bid in. So we did – a silly bid. Anyway, it turns out the lady who was selling it liked David when she'd met us when we'd gone for a little look round. And she believed he could look after her cows and the land properly, so she wanted us to have it. Just like in the UK again.

People must see you as guardians in some way.

I suppose so. Well, anyway, we moved to New Zealand. In fact, we were living over there when David's dad died. He felt very guilty about leaving him, so it was a difficult time for him. He was unsettled, but I did very well over there. I just kept getting offered jobs.

I've done lots of jobs and community work over the years. I was a director on my husband's board and shareholder with his business, so I had a lot of involvement in its development. We actually did a lot of business in Hawaii and America, with new concepts. That's very much what my husband retrained himself to do after farming.

Then I got very involved in a business forum for women. We used to meet locally, once a week, for lunch or dinner and discuss things we thought were important in the community that we could help with. We set up a fund and resources to help those who weren't educated, had left school early, had kids young or were under-privileged – mainly young women but sometimes men too as we didn't discriminate. We'd help them upgrade their education to get their High School Diplomas, assist with childcare, their CVs. We had a section called *Dress for Success* where we'd donate our own clothes or we'd buy stuff for people for interviews and help them with interview practice. We would tap into lots of business resources that we knew about or were involved with to get them jobs. We also developed childcare facilities. It was in its infancy but doing really well.

I also got very involved with young people in a venture called *Sweet Pea Productions*. Three of us set it up: a teaching consultant, a teacher and me. We organised concerts and suchlike, using local talent, including my daughter who's a musician, to showcase people in the arts while raising money for scholarships so they could go to university and study. That's still running today. I'm just a silent partner in that one now.

Then the last project, while we were in New Zealand, was helping women deal with cancer, especially breast cancer, to look good and feel good. We did charity fundraising events, including a big function with a meal and catwalk runway and lots of local designers and even TV involvement. So it was very rewarding.

A woman of many talents.

It was surreal. In New Zealand life was easy for me, and I fitted into life. My daughter was enjoying it over there. It was like stepping back in time. She had a childhood. We did all the things we wanted to, like riding horses. I kept horses and cows. We had calves every year and chickens and all those sort of things. I grew my own vegetables. It was a nice lifestyle.

Then we bought an old nunnery we'd found in Auckland and we practically dug it up, chopped it in half, put it onto articulated lorries and moved it northwards, three hours by road. We then had to put it

> "... life was easy for me, and I fitted into life."

on top of a hill, which was a bit of an art form. The whole town came out to watch it going up the hill. They all thought we were mad. The winch broke and we nearly lost half of it. So we got two bulldozers and more winches and they got it up the hill and we gradually did it up. It was beautiful, with verandas and all colonial style. Perfect. Really, we'd got the perfect life.

Kamila, our daughter, wanted to go to university in London. So she and I were over in England for her auditions when I found a lump in my breast while I was in the shower. I thought it was nothing, but it turned out to be breast cancer that had spread. So I had to make the decision to be treated in England or go back to New Zealand. I decided England was the better option to get the treatment, so I didn't go back home except for one short visit for a wedding. My six-week holiday in England with my daughter ended up being a permanent solution.

"I found a lump … I thought it was nothing, but it turned out to be breast cancer that had spread."

Ironically, when I found out I actually had breast cancer, my house was being used for the big cancer charity event. I said, "Carry on. It doesn't matter. Use the house and whatever." But they felt they couldn't because it was too close to home. It all went ahead successfully at another venue. Then they offered to fundraise because I couldn't get the drug, Herceptin, in New Zealand. In fact, that was one of the reasons I came back to England. They even offered to raise £200,000 for my year's treatment, but I couldn't put that pressure on people. So, as we were still taxpayers in England, we came back.

After seven years in New Zealand, we all moved back here. At first I lived with a friend, Kamila went back to New Zealand to pack her stuff up and David came over to see me through the first couple of operations. Then in the middle of that, my mum was getting remarried because she'd moved to New Zealand with us. So, complete with stitches and everything else, I travelled back for the wedding straight after my operation. We got back to New Zealand on Christmas morning and had a fabulous time with family and friends. Then there was the wedding and off I went back to England. David followed later.

We lived in my sister-in-law's house back in Scrooby for a while. So we'd gone from having everything to living out of a suitcase and then were promoted to the static caravan in the backyard here at the Manor, which, in the meantime we'd inherited. David's brother wanted to do a swap. He didn't want the work involved here at the Manor. So my long-term wish when I first got married, of getting this place, came true.

But the house had been flooded out all through the ground floor, so it was under an inch of water everywhere. David quickly did up the kitchen and the bathroom, while we lived in the static caravan and went back to basics. We had garden furniture in the kitchen that my friends put together with me. There were three girlfriends helping me because David was sorting things out in New Zealand. There was none of our own furniture. Everything was begged and borrowed, and you know, they were some of the happiest times we've ever had.

What do you put that down to?

I think your values change when you come to the crux and you think that life could be cut short here. Not that I ever thought it would be because I always thought cancer was part of my journey – I was very positive. I don't think I had a dull moment throughout the whole thing. I had a few funny ones where the wig would come off at the wrong time and frighten the waiter in the restaurant. Or at the traffic lights, someone would be looking over and I'd get hot and sticky and off would come the wig. My nickname was Bald Eagle because they could all spot me in the shopping centre!

And the cancer now? Is it all... ?

In remission. But I don't really class it as that. It's gone. I have a bit of heart damage, but I live with that and get on with it. So I'm back at work, doing everything normally.

> "I think your values change when you come to the crux and you think that life could be cut short here."

What about your newly married mother who followed you to New Zealand, only for you to return to England?

She had moved reluctantly to New Zealand in the first place. When I had said we were moving there, she said, "Oh no. I've just retired." We'd built her an annex over here – it was beautiful – and then we decided to emigrate. She wasn't very impressed but thought, *Okay, I'm sixty-odd now. I'll go for it.* – which she did, and we all lived together. I don't know how we did it but we did. Then David, Kami and I moved out and she had the original house. And then she found a man, which was lovely because she'd been on her own for twenty years. My dad had died in his forties – he crashed his light aircraft. He always lived life to the full, very energetic, and he left a big, *big* gap. I've always been fortunate in having a very close family. I've had no disasters in my childhood or anything like that – apart from my dad dying prematurely. Very steady, happy, lots of opportunities. When I married into David's family, I suppose that's why I found it so restricting.

[Nodding] A totally different ethos and culture.

Mine were young at heart and his were very old-fashioned and traditional. But they were an older generation as well.

How did your mum end up coming back here?

She remarried during the middle of everything and, bless him, her new husband Graham wasn't well within three months of being married. He developed cancer and it spread to his spine and brain. Within six months, he died. My mum actually nursed him at home until she couldn't do it anymore because he'd lost the function of his legs and his bladder and his bowels. He was only in hospital two weeks before he died. It was quite sad really. It was almost as if they were meant to get married so my mum could care for him as he'd been on his own for a long, long time. Anyway, they had good times together in the short time they had.

After a year, my mum decided she'd rather be with us as a family, so we moved her back in. We made a little room off the kitchen into her bedroom. Last winter she had no electricity apart from an extension wire with a side lamp and a plug-in heater, but she managed. Now, while she's on holiday, we're getting it completely revamped with electricity and a heater. So when she comes home, she can walk into a completely new place.

I'm sure she'll appreciate that. So tell me more about Scrooby Manor.

I knew it had some historical significance because my father-in-law was known as Lord of the Manor. It was like a joke, but I always put it on his birthday cards because he wasn't into that sort of thing. I'd tease him and call him His Lordship. Then I was off work and sitting around, going through chemotherapy, radiotherapy and everything when I moved into the Manor. So I had a lot of time on my hands and started delving into the history. We kept finding things, like old papers, when we were doing it up. So I made a trip to the Nottingham archives.

However, I couldn't read a thing because it was all in Latin. So I asked, tentatively, for help from the local museum and other places, but I didn't get anywhere. Then by chance I was chatting to somebody who did the Pilgrim Father tours. He said, "Well, actually, the lady I run the tours with knows quite a bit about the history."

I said, "She's not, by any chance, called Sue Allan?"

"Yes," he said.

I'd just read one of her books – it relates to the time of the Pilgrim Fathers – because the Pilgrim Fathers were associated with Scrooby Manor. The book was brilliant!

I knew that Sue was doing a book launch at Gainsborough Old Hall about twenty minutes away in Lincolnshire, but David and I were due to go out that night. It was with business associates, not very interesting, and I'd had a hard day at work. So I asked David, "Will you take me to Gainsborough Old Hall? I want to look at it and I'd like to see what Sue's written." He agreed. So I met Sue and we realised we had a passion for the Pilgrims – how it all started and developed. There also seemed to be significant links between Scrooby Manor and the Hall.

> "... going through chemotherapy, radiotherapy and everything ... I had a lot of time on my hands and started delving into the history."

We decided we'd chat over tea and cakes, so she came to the Manor for the first time because it hadn't been opened to the public before. I warned her, "It's in a bit of a mess and it's not what you think it is, but we've got plans for it," and that's how our friendship started. Now we dip in and out of each other's lives in different ways, but we've kept coming back to the history of this place and what it would have been like.

Now we've embarked upon the research – well, mainly Sue because she's got one of those brains – on the Manor's history, how it had come about, who had stayed here, who had owned it and everything else. Of course, I'm a bit of an archaeologist with a Labrador dog. *[Smiling]* Every now and again we find things and I think, *"What's that?"* I was digging at the back and I came across what I thought were two graves. So I covered them up very quickly and said to Sue, "I've found these two stone structures in this shape and when I last saw *Time Team* on TV[1], they said they were graves. So I wasn't quite sure what to do." Every time I found something in the house or outside, Sue would come charging round to have a look. And then we were put into contact with different people who knew more about architectural history so we could do things properly.

---

1   British Channel 4 TV series where archaeology experts investigate a site, usually in the UK, over a three-day dig.

What's lined up next?

The original part of the house – this room we're sitting in now, which we call the music room – was a single storey and part of the original building. As you go southwards from here, you've got the oldest part, probably including the oldest brick you could find in this area. The earliest record I could find was 1207, but there's a lot before that. It was obviously a building of significance and described as an outstanding palace for its time. So it just makes you wonder.

We've got what was probably a three-storey building at the end, which could be a tower – who knows – with a carriage building attached to it. But we're still investigating. We've found old fireplaces. We thought the end room was a chapel, but we can't find the font that was originally seen. One of the old ladies in the village told me where things were in her day when she used to play here. She said the Americans used to come round in the '40s and '50s, and when the farmer was out working, they used to show people round and charge them. That's how they earned their money. She mentioned there was a font in that front room, but we can't find any evidence of it so far because they'd breeze blocked the inner walls to make them straight. We're restoring the walls, using all the proper lime mortar and preserving what we can.

Do you believe it could be the chapel where the Pilgrims would have gathered?

I'm not sure. I'm wondering now if they've reused some carved stonework they found elsewhere. There are records of the original chapel having two organs and that room really isn't big enough to hold anything so huge. I think it was probably part of the living accommodation of the second court, from what Sue and I can gather.

What else do you know about the site?

Well, it's got a huge moat. You can still see it all the way around. The site would have been completely moated. It had an inner wall of a significant size and it was in two courts, according to John Leland, King Henry VIII's historian. We're sitting in the second court, which was usually a quarter of the size of the main court. So it would have been quite a size.

There was a gatehouse and drawbridge – I mean these moats were probably eleven to twelve feet deep at least and the expanse of them was quite significant as well from what I've read. You can see on the south side it's still quite deep. There are outlines of fishponds, so the Manor would have been self-sustaining. We'd like to restore and restock them one day.

When you're digging in the garden, you come across stone foundations. There are lots, which we hope may be significant too, where the modern farm buildings are. Eventually, we'll demolish them and turn the area into grassland so it's more park-like. I'd love to develop a walkway for people to meander through sections and discover where the buildings were, so we can create gardens round the shapes of the Great Hall, Chapel, Great Chamber, Kitchen and Brewhouse.

Apparently, a brick tunnel was found on the village green in the '50s or '60s that came directly from here. You couldn't quite stand up in it, but it was quite wide. We don't know its purpose, but there'll be a huge underground buttery and cellars somewhere still to find.

This is a massive undertaking. What's your vision for Scrooby Manor?

Well, it's a family home but we see ourselves as caretakers and obviously, it would be nice to keep it in the family but I'd also like to share it with others. I think it would have to be in a controlled way because we do have people arrive and dig up the lawn and stand on buildings to take photographs. We've had coachloads of people who have parked in the driveway and not let us out. Things like that. So for now, we allow Sue Allan to do her tours by appointment while it's being done up. It's going to take time.

After talking with the Woodland Trust, we've got a big tree planting project coming up too. They've advised us on what to plant where, according to old records. So we're planting a bank of willow on the southeastern side and covering the concrete from the farm lightly with soil as it is ideal for planting wildflowers.

> "[Scrooby Manor] [is] a family home, but we see ourselves as caretakers ... I'd also like to share it with others."

The soil in the fields is very high quality – too fertile for wildflowers – because the river used to flow around at the back of us where we're sitting now and there was a deer park with oaks.

So, we're going to develop copses and an avenue of trees. Unfortunately, we've got the East Coast train line at the other side of the field, so we're going to screen that off as best we can with evergreen and then plant native trees.

But we've got a lot of wildlife here – badgers, tawny owls, barn owls, buzzards. There's a lot of birdlife because we've got a lot of ground life! *[Laughing]* A local hunter told us he caught a huge black mink a few months ago.

So, yes, the plan is to develop the site, make it look good, and then allow people to come and share it. We'd like to share it with the village sometimes and bring back some of the old traditions like the May Day celebrations and the manorial rights and help them with a visitors' centre in the village. All the money from the tours, which Sue donates to us, goes directly to the church to maintain it.

Some philanthropy from Her Ladyship!

My daughter would like Lady of the Manor on her passport. *[Laughing]* I thought only the title Lord of the Manor existed, but apparently it's a separate title. Apparently, 'Lady of the Manor' is an actual, landed title – the only one left – but until we actually get it out of the local solicitors' vaults, we don't know for certain.

You might be in the House of Lords yet.

[Shaking her head] I don't think so!

Do you have time for any other interests?

I enjoy organising fundraising events. In the middle of chemotherapy, while I had no hair, two friends and I cooked and served a four-course meal for eighty people at a charity dinner. *[Laughing]* It kept me going, kept me positive and gave me something else to think about. Even though I couldn't walk at the end of the night, it didn't matter.

A lot of people could learn from your positive attitude.

I think that's what you need to do – stop feeling sorry for yourself – because there are a lot of people worse off. I also help with Cancer Voices. I review books they're bringing out and run patient groups and workshops. I've also put my name down for some government initiatives to look at cancer outcomes and how we can improve people's lives.

I've actually been a nurse for thirty years now. I started off as a children's nurse, but I've done surgical theatres and intensive care for quite some time. I had a little break, and then I did my medical secretary's course and worked in that role. But somehow I kept slipping back into practice nursing. When I went to New Zealand, I went into intensive care. The problem was that they were putting me on the helicopters and sending me off for all the emergencies and I got very travel sick. I loved it – it was exciting and what I was trained for – but I couldn't cope with the helicopters. Every time it banked, I went green and I couldn't do anything else but be sick.

I eventually left and applied for a nice little job, back in uniform as a nurse, and ended up their Operations Manager – I don't know how. I helped them develop a whole new complex of theatres and consultation rooms. It was all running nicely when unfortunately the man I worked for drowned. He got lost at sea, going back to his yacht, and I couldn't face working there anymore. It just wasn't the same.

Yet again I applied for another *normal* nursing job. I worked for them for a couple of years and they promoted me to Operations Manager! I did *eventually* achieve my goal of being a Nurse Manager.

I've chosen to be back in uniform again now. I work part-time in chronic pain management, doing treatments and things with the consultants. I can now pursue what I love doing – supporting my daughter with her career, my husband with his new inventions and my animals.

It seems you're meant to be the Operations Manager of your life.
It wouldn't be me if I wasn't busy.

It wouldn't be you either if you didn't have an open house.
We take all waifs and strays and, as the sign in the kitchen says, 'Come in as strangers, leave as friends'.

I definitely know from personal experience that that's correct. You're very much a mother, aren't you?
I've found my niche and I want everybody else to succeed and do what they want to do – like yourself. It'd be lovely to see you get your book finished and do all the things you want to do. It's the same with my husband and his invention, my daughter's career and Sue with her books – which I'd love to see turned into films – because people deserve it, and I'll always fight a cause.

That sounds like me. I got arrested fighting a cause, but there we go, that's another story.
I actually got barred from a pub once. Totally out of character. It wasn't because of me. It was my three-year-old daughter. She had a fight with the landlord's son and I got barred from the

"I've found my niche and I want everybody else to succeed and do what they want to do … because people deserve it."

pub. I thought it was brilliant. I don't tell people why I got barred. It just adds character, doesn't it? *[Laughing]*

It does indeed. Anything else I need to know? *[Laughing]*

[Chuckling] No, I'm not telling any more!

I catch up with Julie soon after 25 May, 2013 when Sue Allan's new book In Search of Scrooby Manor *was launched. We laugh as we start the Skype call. I comment on how dreadful I look and Julie says she has not dared put her video on!*

How was the book launch you've just organised? I bet it was amazing.

Yes, it was a busy day. Crikey! It was jam-packed. You couldn't see anything in the Village Hall at all, just a mass of people. All the Americans – forty of them – were fabulous, such characters. It was good to see them because 9/11 had such a negative effect on people coming over. Even the MP made an effort and came out! And the display that Sue and her publisher did was good. We had all these costumes and Henry VIII with his great big codpiece and a projection going through a presentation and morris dancers and a folk band.

Yeah, it was good. The local Pilgrim Fathers pub put on a lunch for the VIPs in the morning, and then all the local ladies rallied round and did cream teas and everything. I was quite surprised. *[Laughs]* When you organise anything, you don't know quite what's going to happen, do you?

Even the vicar came in all her garb. She's a bit like the 'Vicar of Dibley'.[2] She did 'Beating of the Bounds' round the croft and the church with rosemary and water. She said, *[mimicking her voice]* "I'm going to make it up as I go along, but I'll do a proper service," *[both laughing]* and then she tucked into a big cream scone. We had a lot of good feedback and lots of people offering help and funding. They're all interested in our new tourist information.

Tell me about that.

On the pub site there's a big barn and outbuildings at the back, which we'd like to lease for twenty-five years minimum and apply for Heritage Lottery funding in a big way.

You see, in the present climate the government's looking at ways of reducing spending and tourism hasn't been a priority for a while. But I think they're missing the point if we don't do anything with tourism in our region. We've got a vast amount of history that is very much untapped. They just use the myth of Robin Hood, which was just a fairy tale. We've got a real, live history here about the Pilgrims and their journey. The people that came from here actually set up America, the First Amendment and everything. It's huge! The 400th anniversary is coming up in seven years. I do know there are very important people coming over from America in 2015 and then again in seven years. Whoever *one* of those important people may be, I can't really say but you can guess.

So if we want to be part of it, we need to organise things now. Doncaster Council is even offering an education centre just down the road that we can use and turn into a native village and do all sorts of things there for kids and education. So, really it's escalating. We've had press in The

---

2   British sitcom starring Dawn French as the Vicar of the rural parish of Dibley.

Times, The Telegraph, Yahoo News. The word's getting out about the Pilgrims and they are all squabbling about who has the rights to the tourism bits, but really it's here.

Can you give me any snippets from the book?

There are some lovely stories about why Scrooby Manor went into disrepair, and the relationship obviously was Catholicism versus Protestantism, which was yo-yoing for a few years. The Archbishops were locked in the Tower of London. They'd had wives and then they had to ditch them. You'll have to read the book to find some interesting facts about who stayed – such as several monarchs – and who didn't and why it was important, and then, obviously, it runs into the Pilgrim story anyway.

So, we are driving the new tourism building and everything that goes with it, and we'll get people wanting to help anyway. We even thought about a memorial garden here so descendants can have either a rose or a tree planted in memory of their relatives and something they can visualise when they come over.

That's a super idea!

I'd like to restore the ponds and the moat, so there's somewhere to walk round. It's starting to look attractive now, but there's not enough to see. You could have a bit of a garden and see the moat, so visitors can visualise what it would have been like. It would bring history back a bit. I mean, looking at a few foundation ruins doesn't do it for me, to be honest. I like somewhere I can stroll through and imagine how life would have been. I mean, we're the devil if we do and the devil if we don't. It's still our home, so we've got to balance things properly. If people understand, we'll be sensitive and allow people over in a structured way. But it won't be an open gate, come when you like, willy-nilly sort of thing. It's a good job that David and I are interested in history and are willing to caretake. One of the big questions people kept asking was, "Do you realise the spiritual significance of your place? You are so privileged." I didn't realise that until I had met so many people who've cried here and sang here. A lady got on the kitchen table to touch the beam in the kitchen with tears streaming down her face. I live here and to me it's a lovely, old rambling cottage, a bit of history.

Yes, I can see it _is_ a spiritual home for millions of Americans.

It's part of _our_ heritage too as they were English to start with. It was _our_ future too. Time to stop separating us off. We are actually one of the same people. It's just some lived abroad and made their lives in a new country.

> "[Scrooby Manor]'s part of our heritage too as they were English to start with. ... Time to stop separating us off. We are actually one of the same people. It's just some lived abroad and made their lives in a new country."

Absolutely. You're right.

In the couple of days I was putting the displays up in the village, there were twenty people just wandering around the village, trying to find out a bit more about the history, and they were English; they weren't Americans. They were from Birmingham and Lancaster, different places, and I was thinking, *Crikey, if people were more aware then we would have a lot more happening here.*

My vision is to see a hub of things happening here. I don't believe in boundaries – like the different counties. It's a community. So there's lots happening and now all the research is finished, it's left me with a bit of a gap – but it was a wonderful journey. You learn so much. My only curiosity is about where Mary Brewster came from. Until we can find extra records that went missing, it may be one of those things that will be left to interpretation. It's all exciting stuff … and I've got myself a new job as well!

Don't tell me. You're managing again!

Well, a friend asked me if I was interested in going back into management. To cut a long story short I got a clinical manager role – in pain management still. I'm getting quite excited but scared at the same time. I was very honest with them about my health problems. And I threw in lots of new ideas to try and think outside the box about what they could do in the future. I didn't go on about all the usual NHS stuff. So they quite liked that.

Excellent. And how is your health, Julie?

Really good! I had my gallbladder whipped out and I feel tons better.

Fantastic!

I'm also doing some work with the Jumbulance Trust. They do wonderful buses with medical equipment and staff it with volunteer nurses, doctors, occupational therapists and the like. We can take the disabled and unwell on holiday with their main carer and fulfil their wishes. I've been helping fundraise and I shall be going on their next holiday. I feel quite strongly that we forget these people. They don't have holidays. They don't have respite very often and it just brings so much pleasure to a few, and I think it needs to grow.

On another good note, Kam's first professional engagement when she's finished at the Guildhall is at St. Paul's Cathedral for the London Handel Festival[3], as a soloist with the English Chamber Orchestra. It has blown her away. She's got a proper contract and everything. Talk about a coup for her first engagement.

How exciting. You must be a very proud mum. What a successful time this is for you all.

Julie for me is the archetypical mother. It seems deep within her nature to be nurturing and supportive of everyone around her, whether she knows them personally or not, or if they have two legs or four. That care extends to the environment – the house she lives in, the land surrounding it, the history beneath her feet. Yet she is so modest about herself and her considerable achievements

---

3   Guildhall School of Music and Drama, London, one of the world's leading conservatoires and drama schools.

that it takes a considerable amount of delving to discover some of her stories. I have a feeling there may be plenty more for another occasion.

When I asked Julie if I could interview her for my book, she was happy to contribute but responded with genuine surprise that she had no idea why. I strongly suspect her motivation in saying 'yes' was to support me and bring Scrooby Manor's story to the world rather than her own.

I chose Julie because as far as I am concerned she is every inch a Pilgrim Mother. She is exactly the person I would want on my side, in my team, within my family, fighting my corner. I know Julie would be right there in the thick of it. She has lots of energy and drive; she is a brilliant organiser at home, at work, for charities and in the community; plus she's fantastic fun!

Like the *Mayflower* Pilgrim Mothers, Julie set off with her family to carve out a successful new life in New Zealand. It was an ironic twist of fate that just seven years later brought her back to England – and to Scrooby Manor in particular. Julie was obviously much loved by the New Zealand community. They even offered to raise £200,000 for her cancer treatment so she could stay, but Julie gracefully declined.

For every setback, Julie welcomed in the corresponding gift. When the family had to sell the farm, Julie saw it as an opportunity for a new life. She viewed cancer positively as part of her journey. I have never heard a word of complaint from Julie. Her whole attitude to life is light-hearted.

What I especially love about Julie is how motherly she is without being 's-motherly'. It is wonderful to offer support – but not subjugate yourself to others. I have at times observed overprotective mothers (and fathers) who don't allow their children any scope for a spirit of adventure to develop. I believe that clinging to your children and living through them is the sign of an unfulfilled, unhealthy and unsustainable life. It is important for modern Pilgrim Mothers to be complete in themselves, comfortable in their own skin and aligned with who they are. Julie's daughter, Kami, is a talented musician who is blessed with her mother's (and father's) support, but they also have their own lives.

Julie talks of having now found her space, her niche. How appropriate that she is living in the actual home of an original Pilgrim Mother, Mary Brewster. As I sat with Julie, I could feel Mary's presence and her pleasure that Julie had taken on *her* mantle as the Lady of Scrooby Manor. I picture Mary smiling approvingly as Julie breathes new life once more into the Brewster family's old home, ready to welcome pilgrims from near and far, inspired by Mary and her fellow Pilgrims' story.

"It is important for modern Pilgrim Mothers to be
complete in themselves, comfortable in their own skin
and aligned with who they are."

JANE NOBLE KNIGHT

KATHERINE WOODWARD THOMAS

"I lead from what's going to be of service to create the greatest amount of goodness and the greatest amount of connectivity and the greatest amount of love. It's about what's going to evolve us forward."

Katherine Woodward Thomas, MA, MFT, is the best-selling author of *Calling in "The One"*. Katherine is a licensed psychotherapist, co-creator of the Feminine Power transformative courses for women, co-creator and co-host of the *Women on the Edge of Evolution* teleseries, and creator of the Conscious Uncoupling Process. Since 2004 Katherine has taught over 200,000 people worldwide, both in person and virtually in the learning communities she co-created with her teaching partner of seven years, Claire Zammit PhD (c). Katherine was born in New York and now lives in Los Angeles. She has one daughter.

www.katherinewoodwardthomas.com

A Conversation with
Katherine Woodward Thomas

Feminine Powerhouse

In common with many people worldwide, Marianne Williamson has been one of my icons since I first read the passage beginning *Our deepest fear*. Following Marianne led to my discovery of other American spiritual teachers, such as Jean Houston, Barbara Marx Hubbard and Craig Hamilton.

In May 2010, Craig emailed information about a Feminine Power teleseminar facilitated by his wife, Claire Zammit, and Katherine Woodward Thomas. It sounded right up my street. Soon afterwards I tuned in to listen. Wow! Katherine and Claire's teachings absolutely blew me away. I was instantly hooked and signed up for the very first Feminine Power programme in June 2010. It was to be a transformative experience.

Impressed, I went on to read Katherine's best-selling book, *Calling in "The One"* – several times! It was equally insightful. In December 2011, I found myself once more enthralled by Katherine's teleseminar on *Conscious Uncoupling*. Initially, I was shocked to hear she and her husband had divorced, but as she spoke I relaxed and understood. Katherine spoke about how unusual it is to divorce amicably. It certainly is, but luckily my ex-husband and I divorced on friendly terms after thirty-plus years of marriage. Even though I wasn't sure I needed it, I enrolled in this programme too; I loved Katherine's work so much I didn't want to miss out on anything she had to share.

When I drew up my Pilgrim Mothers wish list for this book, Katherine's name was one of the first I recorded. Now bear in mind, I am a huge fan, so it was like asking a film star or a top media personality to be in my book. Although I felt slightly apprehensive, I took the view, 'If you don't ask, you don't get'.

So, on Friday, 30 December 2011, after the family Christmas celebrations were over, I spent the day composing and then sending an email to Katherine outlining what I was doing and making my request. I surmised that a gatekeeper would decide if my request was worthy of Katherine's attention. I was thrilled when seven hours later, on New Year's Eve no less, I had a personal reply from Tina Conte, in Katherine's Course Liaison Team. We exchanged further emails and a phone call on the evening of New Year's Day. I had really not expected anyone to be working that weekend. I was ecstatic when the next morning – again a bank holiday – I had a beautiful email from Katherine, expressing *her honour* to be one of my Pilgrim Mothers. Words are inadequate to describe my feelings of elation. Katherine's positive response to me was the greatest confirmation I could have received that I was meant to write this book.

The 'much in demand' Katherine has suggested we speak on President's Day, her best chance of having unbroken time with me. At 6 pm my time, and 10 am Katherine's, I sit at my kitchen table, ready for our Skype call – laptop in front, copious neon-highlighted notes to my left and right, and multi-coloured post-its decorating the wall to my right. As soon as Katherine speaks, I feel like I am talking with a close friend. Her tone is consistently warm, calm and soothing, despite having to continue with some work on a holiday and printing off documents in the background.

I relax into her familiar honey-toned voice, totally ignore my notes and lose myself in the conversation…

Thank you for this opportunity to learn more about your story, Katherine.

I think what you're creating is so beautiful, Jane. You're an inspiration to women. I read a couple of years back – it was a great validation to my instincts – that people really need role models of people who have done it in order to embody change and move forward in life. Concepts alone or insights alone are not enough. So, what you are doing is providing role models.

Thank you. I've reached sixty, an age where many women, particularly in the media, can become invisible. In fact, they may have been invisible for some time. I want to redress the balance because there is so much wisdom to be gained from older women.

I also think you have the eros that is inspiring you each day. [1] Our culture doesn't really encourage that in women. There's a big reclamation going on and you're evidence of that. So when a woman is creative and is, as Barbara Marx Hubbard calls it, 'vocationally aroused', she's attractive and visible again, no matter what her age.

Barbara's a great role model. And yourself, Katherine...

Thank you. I will be fifty-five this summer myself.

You don't look it. What you're spreading globally is absolutely amazing. When you were setting out in life, did you have any sense of a life mission, a calling?

I had a sense, when I was probably about fourteen years old, that I wanted to devote my life to the evolution of love in the world. It's a very young age, but what happened was that even though I was born into a rather unreligious home, when I was fourteen, I started to have spontaneous, spiritual experiences where I was kind of transported. I had experiences in my body where I felt the presence of God. I don't know how else to describe it. It started with a Christian experience in a little church service where I had gone into a Sunday School class, and this woman was speaking about God.

At this age, I was already quite jaded and acting out. I had boyfriends, I was smoking cigarettes

---

1   Eros: This is our creative life instinct that drives our acts of self-preservation and growth, leading to uninhibited enjoyment of life. Often associated with sexual drive – a zest for life.

and drinking wine, and I was just very, very precocious. So I was arguing with her, but by the end of the conversation, I said a prayer. I wasn't expecting anything, but the moment I said the prayer, this energy washed through my body and I just felt this warmth and this light. I had never heard of an experience like that before, so it was quite genuine. I didn't even know that that was in the realm of human possibility. Certainly, I was unaware that anyone in this church was having that kind of experience, so it was very eye-opening for me.

That experience started me on a spiritual path. I knew there was a higher power and that I was supposed to devote my life to this higher power. Soon after that, I would start to 'commune' with this energy. I remember one morning specifically, when I was in ninth grade, I was walking to school – I was a little late, so I was alone on my walk – and I suddenly started to have this transcendent experience where I saw what it would be like for our entire world, the population of humanity, to be completely awakened to the energy of interconnectivity and care in our relationships with each other, extending relatedness and warmth and taking on the wellbeing of the whole. In that moment, I saw the possibility of what it is to be human, both individually and collectively, and I just said yes to it. I knew that that was my calling in life.

> "I saw the possibility of what it is to be human, both individually and collectively, and I just said yes to it. I knew that that was my calling in life."

So consequently, I had a rough time in life because I think for most of us who make ourselves available to that sense of purpose and say yes to the evolutionary impulse of life that's wanting to bring something new into being and 'up-level' the game for all of us, that journey is going to be the descent into hell ... That's often the experience that those of us who are here to be of service begin with. We have to go into the very bottom of the human experience in order to bring light there. It's one thing to talk about the light, but it's another thing if you're having an experience of light and you try and describe it to someone who's not, who's in the darkness. And it's another thing again to actually go into the darkness and then find your way out by discovering the light within you, one step at a time, so that you're then able to lead people out of the darkness with you.

That's been my journey. I descended into very bad food addiction. I say 'bad food addiction,' but I was really non-functional for about twelve years of my life. A lot of heart-breaking things happened: my father disappeared from my life; I was estranged from my family; and my boyfriend, who I had all through high school and was planning on marrying, married someone else and severed me off. All sorts of things happened, one after another after another, which threw me into a dark night of the soul that lasted many years.

When I was going through all of that, I thought that God had abandoned me because I had had a spiritual practice before then. I had started spiritual practice when I was fifteen. I had read the Bible from cover to cover by the time I was eighteen, two times. I just wanted to. I was hungry for spiritual sustenance. And it was funny because I was hanging out with all the druggies in school, and they would be doing drugs while I would be sitting and reading the Bible. I'd tell them all about what I'd been learning, and then I'd smoke a cigarette with them. *[Laughing]*

I went to Bible School when I was nineteen because I wanted to be a missionary and devote my life to doing good works in the world. My family was appalled, and that's when I became estranged from them. They threw me out because I wasn't following the path they thought was the right path. I'm sure I was rebellious and bratty and all sorts of things to my mother; she has her own version of that story.

> "I was hungry for spiritual sustenance."

But basically, when I was nineteen, I ended up having a nervous breakdown because so many difficult and challenging things happened in my life. I sometimes laugh and say that I was a Bible School dropout! At the time, I was in so much pain that I thought God had abandoned me. I thought it was all for naught. Life was very lonely and frightening. I had very addictive patterns and was deeply isolated and alone, and I had this anxiety disorder. I became agoraphobic and I couldn't leave my house. I was living in poverty. I had several, very dark years and finally, when I was in my mid-twenties, I discovered the *12 Step Programme*. It was a very funny thing because, you know, that programme is a spiritual programme and you need to pray. I had stopped praying because I was so angry and just assumed that life had abandoned me and that somehow my prayers were not answered. I had thought when I went to Bible School that I was going to have a beautiful life of service and devotion, and then everything turned into this very dark journey. So, I had stopped praying, basically as an act of rebellion and anger.

But of course in the *12 Step Programme* you have to pray, so my first prayer in several years was "Okay, well, I have to talk to you. So, my prayer is *F*** You!*" *[Lots of laughing]*

But it got God and me talking again. A funny thing was that I had to forgive God – isn't that silly? – in order to move forward and recover. So we got over that hurdle, and I did recover. It took me a long time. I was doing 12 Step work, I was in therapy and I started doing transformative workshops; I just began to organise my life around my own recovery and development. That was pretty much life for a long time.

I was somewhat under-realised. I was a singer at the time. I loved singing, and it helped me to heal and recover, but I couldn't make a living at it. So I was doing things that I didn't like. I waitressed for years and I was working as a temp legal secretary, which was a rather thankless and isolated job because when you went into places, you were just a temp, so no one would bond with you, really. If you did bond, you would be leaving in a few days so it was a very under-actualised experience, truthfully. Still, I was working on myself.

For about twelve years, I had that kind of life. But I worked very hard to think creatively about my life and appreciate what I did have, even though I was still going through a lot of hard times. Then, by about thirty-four or thirty-five, I was actually healed from the eating disorder. I was so grateful, Jane, that I prayed and I said to Life, "You did this beautiful thing for me. What can I do for you?" I truly meant it, and I really listened. I was very unhappy. I didn't have a love in my life, I didn't have work that I loved and I didn't have money. But I just made up my mind that if love was not going to come to me, I was going to go to love and I was going to create love; I was going to generate it.

This was the early '90s. I didn't know what to do. I wanted to do something beautiful and deeply good as an offering to life, as an expression of gratitude for having recovered. So it was very wholesomely motivated, and I sat with that question for about six weeks without needing to rush it. It was really a very serious enquiry. Six weeks in, I was out jogging on the side of the road and it came to me in a flash what I was supposed to do. I just knew it in an instant…

There were a lot of homeless people in Los Angeles and people were feeling very burdened in their hearts by this phenomenon of panhandling at the freeway entrance. As a singer and a songwriter and a musician, I certainly knew the power of music to heal, so I had this idea. I was going to go down to Skid Row and I was going to create a format for people to be able to co-write songs about their lives and make a CD of it. I felt it; I knew it was perfect. I cried … I was so moved by the whole idea.

> "… I just made up my mind that if love was not going to come to me, I was going to go to love and I was going to create love. I was going to generate it."

I immediately got into action. I had zero idea of how to make that happen, but I put one foot in front of the other and followed my instincts. I ended up getting a partner on the project who *did* know how to make something like that happen. We went down and met with people at one of the missions. We have rehab centres on Skid Row here in Los Angeles and one of them, the Los Angeles Mission, gave me a group of eighteen men and women to work with. We started to do writing workshops, which gave them an opportunity to tell their story of recovery and hope. We prepared them to work with professional songwriters who were coming to co-write songs about healing from getting off the streets. I ended up having world class Grammy winners and Emmy nominees – just amazing songwriters. Of course, I *was* in LA with some of the best songwriters in the world and everybody loved the project.

What happened was I was meeting with these eighteen men and women and the partner I had taken on was completely empowering the structures to make this happen. I was a singer-songwriter and a temp secretary; I had been a waitress for years and had no training. But I knew intuitively how to craft a programme for them that was very transformative in nature. I started to run these little creative writing workshops over a series of about four weeks, and in this time these people's whole lives were transforming.

I had an epiphany in one of those workshops that brought me to my knees. What I realised was that these people were transforming because of what I knew from my own experience and because I had had a transmission of what it was to come from the darkest of nights and to find your way into the light. So the transmission was speeding up their process. They were weeping and having tremendous breakthroughs. In fact, I tracked those people for the next five years and I had something like an eighty per cent success rate of people staying off the streets, which is unheard of.

I designed this whole collaborative programme with people coming in and writing with these mission writers as equal share collaborators. The mission writers were not the recipients of charity. They were the ones who were actually donating the proceeds from their song to the mission that had helped them to turn their lives around. So it was actually an identity shift into part of the solution.

So, it was very comprehensive, and I just knew intuitively how to do this. The epiphany was "Oh, my gosh. Going into the darkness was not God abandoning me; it was actually the answer to my prayer." That's when I understood who I was and what I came here to create and what I had to offer. I went back to school to become a therapist to give me the credentials to actually work with people, and that was a seven-year journey.

That music project ran for five years in the LA music community – it was really moving. People not only wrote songs with their professional writers, they went into the studio and recorded them. Then we had a concert in the community where their story was presented to the community at large. People gave standing ovations to welcome them back into the community. It was a very, very moving, touching project. It was very beautiful. It just generated something that was *so loving.*

And that's *the creative impulse* that I want to point out. There are so many times when we want to step up and do something, but there are so many things that are off in how we are living that need to be rectified. It's very easy to become consumed with what we're against. I think the creative process needs *to be* what it is that it's aiming for; it has to be generating that. Basically, the *In Harmony with the Homeless* project generated a lot of love in the world where there wasn't love. It was a whole new thing, and it was deeply moving and actually worked. It transformed people's lives for good; it really changed them. That experience changed everybody who was touched by that process.

When I became a therapist, I had my own experience with calling in love. I had trouble in that area for so many years. So when I was able to create that for myself – I was single at forty, married at forty-one, pregnant at forty-two, had my first child at forty-three, and I was so grateful for that I decided to make another offering. And this was to track the process that I had gone through to manifest love; to release the obstacles that I had in the way to being able to have a marriage and be a mother and create that experience for myself. Out of that, *Calling in "The One"* was born. I wrote that book really as an offering.

Again, it had a lot of destiny to it. As I was writing it I didn't know anything about the business of getting books published. But my focus was really on being helpful, making an offering, which is very important – for me anyway. I try and think from a very wholesome, motivated place – never in terms of "What's going to make money?" first. Those of us who have a great passion or a longing to have an impact for good in the world do have to think about money, to think about marketing, because that's how we get our message out; I always say if Jesus came back now, he'd have to be very good at sound bites. *[Laughing]* I had to learn how to do that because of my distaste for marketing. I had the idea that marketing was manipulation, but I know now that if you're marketing, it's just messaging and it's a form of love too. It's an offering of love.

> "If you're marketing … it's a form of love too. It's an offering of love."

So, it's important to market, but I never lead from that. I do my best to lead from what's going to be of service to create the greatest amount of goodness and the greatest amount of connectivity and the greatest amount of love. It's about what's going to evolve us forward. That's generally where Claire, my teaching partner, and I are coming from, and that's how we created the Feminine Power work together and how we actually bonded. It was really over that kind of wholesome motivation and that fervour to bring forth things of goodness and care into the world.

How did you get your book published?

As I was writing *Calling in "The One"*, I was having dinner with friends and one was a trainer. He said, "I hear you're writing. Do you need an agent?"

I replied, "Well probably ... I guess." I hadn't really thought of it.

He said, "Well, I'm training this agent and I'd be happy to give her something." I didn't know how to write a book proposal, and frankly I didn't really want to write it because I was busy writing the first chapter of the book. So in a way it was a distraction to me. But I thought, okay, well he offered, so I put together a schlocky, half-hearted book proposal, and I attached the first chapter I'd just written. About two months later, this agent called me and said, "You know what? Your book proposal is so bad, but the first chapter of your book has changed my life." *[Laughing]* She said, "I was in this barren place. I had no love in my life and I read your first chapter. And now I have this amazing relationship. I'll take you on if you'll hire someone to help you with a book proposal," which I did. So, that's how *Calling in "The One"* was born. I had no platform, no writing credits; it was the first thing I'd ever written. And I wasn't even looking for a book deal.

We got a deal with Random House, and it's funny because later on people were saying, "Oh, my gosh! You got a book deal with Random House? How did that happen? That is so hard. I've been trying for years." I just look at them and think, *Thank you so much for not telling me that. [Laughing]* Had I known it was so hard, I may not have done it. I think we want to be mindful of the impact our words have on each other and always look to inspire one another, rather than kill off the creative impulses we all have towards contribution, creativity and care.

So to answer your other question, Jane, did I know I had a calling? Yes, I can't recall the first time I knew but it was about twenty years ago. I knew I was going to be a transformative teacher. I don't know how I knew. It wasn't necessarily an ambition – it was a calling. I didn't know how it would fulfil itself, but I do recall that my orientation to my own personal growth and development was to prepare. And I find that that's actually my orientation even now, after having arrived in the land of milk and honey, having the fulfilment of being where I am, privileged to be teaching tens of thousands of people and having an impact. But even when one arrives at the land of milk and honey – as we all know – there are imperfections in life; there are unfulfilled desires and problems and breakdowns. And so the main question is: What is the right relationship to life? Whether you're fulfilled or you're not fulfilled, what is the right relationship to our longing? And my answer today to that question is that it's a developmental relationship. The longing is always the food of creation.

> "It's living from the future as opposed to living from the past. Most of us are living our lives referenced from our past."

I find a lot of times things will happen to me now and I'll go "Gosh, I've manifested this. I wanted it three years ago, but I don't even know if I want it that much anymore." So I find there's sometimes a little lag time. I mean sometimes there's like the parking lot experience where it's like "Oh here it is." *[Laughing]* But for the most part, we're always generating the future. And I think if any of you look back over what you were thinking twenty years ago, you're now living the fulfilment of that. And certainly, my life is the fulfilment of what I wanted ten, twenty, thirty years ago. Of course, now I have different longings.

That's what is bringing us to the creative process all the time – these endless yearnings, this endless awareness of new hungers that we have now.

But to have a developmental relationship we have to think like this: "Okay great, that's where I'm going, so how do I want to be preparing today? What's required of me today in order to become the woman I would need to be to manifest that future?" It's living from the future as opposed to living from the past. Most of us are living our lives referenced from our past. We're running away from something, we're trying to fix something; we're trying to heal something. But we're identified with the sense of self that we developed when we were young, and we're trying to improve upon that or expand upon that.

I find it's very beautiful and valuable and even, in many ways, more powerful to be living according to the future that we're yearning to create. We then allow that future to determine our actions and choices, what we're thinking about, and how we're oriented around our own deficits and where we want to be growing. So, I have a very developmental relationship to life which is, I think, the right relationship, certainly for a teacher. And so there's actually no place of arriving at success.

I think the definition of success is going to be different according to which part of the self you identify with. What I mean by that is that if you're identified with the egoic self, the definitions of success are going to be the accomplishments or the accoutrements, the accolades, that you're able to create, the position in life – those kinds of things. Like you're married, you have a family, you have a book out in the world, you have a project that was picked up, you have a successful business, you have to hit certain markers or numbers, or whatever that is. That's one definition of success.

When you're looking from a soul level at what success is, it's very different criteria. Success might be walking through the temptation of accomplishment and accolades and still keeping your motivation wholesome. Success is also being willing to be true to one's calling, even if that means disappointing other people, turning away from what people would expect. It's about living a more true life. It's about self-honesty; deep authenticity with where one needs to grow. It's about being able to continue to grow in humility and with grace. Success from a soul level, from a real depth level of who one really is, is always going to be about living a life of truth, goodness, contribution and beauty, no matter what the externals look like – no matter what!

> "Success from a soul level, from a real depth level of who one really is, is always going to be about living a life of truth, goodness, contribution and beauty, no matter what the externals look like – no matter what!"

That's so beautiful and insightful, Katherine.

Thank you... So, my definition of success is to not be owned, even now, by the worldly success that I have; to be true to my own calling and my devotion to serving the evolution of love in the world. To keep my heart just as wholesomely motivated as I was when I was fourteen and I had that original vision. I'm so grateful for having found my purpose so young because when you're a teenager, you can love in a very pure way. You're not captured by the machinery of all the things that we're involved in as grown-ups. So a very pure home base is within me, and this is where I can revert to when I get overwhelmed or confused or distracted or tempted. When I lose my footing and I get egoically based, I can go back to that moment and remember who I am and what I really belong to.

I also want to say one more thing about this because I am loving the opportunity to share this with people. I know that so many of us are yearning for an authentic life right now, and that's the deepest yearning – for an authentic life and a life of contribution – and I hope it's helpful to some ... When *Calling in "The One"* came out, I definitely knew it had a big calling and a big destiny. I remember the book company not really taking me seriously because I was an unknown author; they assumed that I didn't know what I was doing. I had to write this press release and I remember telling the book publisher, "But you have to get the wording right because hundreds of thousands of people are going to hear this story." She literally laughed and blew it off. To her, I was probably just another crazy author who had delusions of grandeur. But I had a *knowing*.

Calling in "The One" has not sold hundreds of thousands of copies yet, so maybe I was a little crazy. But it has actually been before tens of thousands of people and really impacted people's lives in a much bigger way than the book company ever expected it to. *[Laughing]* Right now, they're just completely shocked and blown away, and they're writing me, saying, "When are you writing another book?" – which is really flattering to me. *[Laughing]*

> "Dear God, please do not let me get known faster than my heart can actually expand to authentically care about people."

But when the book came out, even though I had that knowing, I said this prayer: "Dear God, please do not let me get known faster than my heart can actually expand to authentically care about people." It's a terrible thing when people become celebrities in a way that disconnects them from others. But those of us who are here as teachers, as lovers of life and way-showers, as you yourself are, know that the best things that we ever bring forward are those that we do so because of love and a desire to alleviate suffering and to unleash creative potentials.

Thank you, Katherine, for those wise words. It explains so well where you're coming from and brings in all sorts of other nuances to do with celebrity as well.

You're welcome. And I know you're a sister, so it's really wonderful to be able to share this with you.

And how did the 'Feminine Power' course and your partnership with Claire come together, Katherine?

I had opened a centre in Los Angeles and was renting out office space. Claire came as a graduate student to rent one of the offices. She felt intuitively it was time for her to start working with people. By that time she had over a decade of study behind her. She was well on her way to getting her PhD in Transformative Education and was developing many of her own ideas about collective intelligence and how to form learning communities – cutting edge ideas.

I was an experienced psychotherapist who had been participating in highly transformative work for many years. So when we met, the combination – the synergy – between us was extraordinary.

Pretty much from the moment we met, we had an instant affinity and just started spending time together. I so enjoyed her. The thing about Claire is that she has very similar sensibilities to what I've just been talking about; she just wanted to be of service. So we started collaborating. I was actually overwhelmed at the time because my book had gone onto the LA Times best-seller list. I had lots of students coming to me and this centre to run.

At first Claire started working with me on the *Calling In "The One"* work. She took over running and managing the classes, as well as being in the room and supporting students. They were all taught live and in person at the time. I saw the contribution she was making in the classes – the level of brilliance and depth that she brought to the conversation. I was so impressed.

Almost immediately, I invited her in to co-teach *all* the classes. I had an intuitive sense about her having a very, very big contribution to make to the world, and I wanted to be of service to her too. Basically, we were feeding each other support and power to realise our full potentials for contribution right from the beginning of our relationship. It became a very collaborative, synergistic process.

At some point, after knowing each other a few months, I had this feeling that I needed to let go of working so hard to get *Calling in "The One"* out in the world and just spend time with Claire. I rebelled against that for about two weeks because it felt premature. I didn't feel secure with *Calling in "The One"* in the world. My mind was telling me I couldn't afford to take time off, but I've learned to really trust that knowing. Even though it didn't make sense to me, and it was in the opposite direction of what I would've thought, I decided to trust the impulse, put all of my busy work aside and started hanging out with Claire, spending a lot of time together. Within a relatively short period of time, our shared fascination with what creates embodied change started to birth the Feminine Power teachings.

It first came into being as a class we offered our students and graduates of *Calling in "The One"*, and we didn't even know what the class was. We just knew that the women who were succeeding at *Calling in "The One"* fairly easily were women who knew how to create things from their feminine, and the women who were having a harder time were women who were much more steeped in masculine ways of knowing and being and thinking. You see *Calling in "The One"* is the Law of Attraction. It's a very feminine, creative process of magnetising things into your life.

We decided to offer a six-week course on feminine energy. We didn't know what we were going to teach because we wanted to get together with the women and see where the women were at. So we couldn't actually create a syllabus yet. We had no name, no bullet points, no promo. We sent out emails to maybe 500 women who were graduates of our courses, and within a week the class filled up, which shocked us. As I said, we didn't even have a name for the class.

"Women were hungry to embrace more feminine qualities; however, they were mistrustful because they thought of feminine as weak and they saw it as a loss of power."

We went into that first class going, "Okay, there's something here, but what is it? The hunger is there." The first night of the class, we saw immediately what the dilemma was. It was this dilemma about *power*. Women were hungry to embrace more feminine qualities; however, they were mistrustful because they thought of feminine as weak and they saw it as a loss of power.

We realised that if you look up the word 'power' in the dictionary, you'll find it defined exclusively in masculine terms: to do, to act, to will, command, to have control over others. We began the enquiry into what power in the feminine looks like; the power that is not about conquering the externals of life; the power that is actually sourced from that which is invisible and that which is internal; the power of *relatedness* – to be able to relate to ourselves so much so that we would have the power to change our own lives; the power to be so related to each other that we would be able to collaborate and co-create the future of our world, to reflect the values of those things that we care most deeply about.

It's about the values of goodness and caring and wellbeing for all, and the power to realise our highest destiny, which is this relationship to life that is very highly creative and generative. And then how to actually create and bring forth the unmanifested potentials that are present for ourselves and for our world. It's not a linear process. It's not something that one can create with a strategic plan. It requires this deep relatedness to the creative energies of life.

That's basically what started to happen, and then immediately we had students and the Feminine Power series was born. The centre became the incubator, and for five years we worked there with several hundred women, developing and teaching before we went to a format on the Internet and created a telecourse. We actually capped the first telecourse we did at a thousand women. More than a thousand wanted to join, but we would only take a thousand. And then two months later, we did another one because we had so many women. We got another thousand women to that telecourse, and that was about a year and a half ago at this point. Several thousand women have taken the seven-week introductory programme. Tens of thousands have listened to the free programme that we offer, and it's been very, very exciting.

I was on that first global telecourse in June 2010, and I remember I made a note of something Claire mentioned. In the first wave of the women's movement in the US in the 1850s, there were a thousand women gathered for the National Conference for Women and that was unheard of. Then in 1966, a thousand women joined the National Organisation for Women, and then in 2010, you had a thousand women who joined your Feminine Power telecourse. Did you feel like pioneers at the time? Was there this sense of making history?

Yes, I have to say that we did feel like pioneers, and I still do feel like a pioneer, although I think pioneering is glamorous in some moments and then very unglamorous most of the time. Probably ninety per cent of pioneering, most of the time, is pretty unglamorous.

What do you mean by that, Katherine?

It's a lot of digging in the trenches. There's the impulse and there's the 'yes' to the impulse – the creative impulse – and the impulse of questing and curiosity and bringing something new forward. And then there's the management of the day to day showing up and the effort required to birth that possibility into the world. In the last several months, we've probably been in a more unglamorous relationship to it, which is the 'heavy lifting'. Just as our grandmothers laboured on those covered wagons, there's mud to be slogged through.

It's all good, but it is what it is. I like to talk about that part because I think it's confusing. I think we're very confused, Jane, around this idea of 'do what you love and the money will follow' because when things get difficult or when effort needs to be made, we'll very often give up and see that as a sign of what must be *not* meant to be. Whereas anything of merit and true value that is brought into our world is brought in with effort. Babies are *pushed* at great cost through that little birth canal. How one births a baby is a great metaphor for how one brings anything of beauty and goodness forward. The creative process has beauty all throughout, and there's nothing wrong with hard work and effort. We want to be careful to not be lazy.

A lot of us get stopped because we say, "Oh, I'm afraid to be visible." We have like a cellular memory of the witch hunts. In our past and in many portions of the world right now, women are oppressed and punished, stoned, tortured and killed because they are too vibrant, too filled with the eros of existence. It's troublesome for women, so we get afraid. We get women saying, "I'm scared, I'm scared," and the answer is courage.

> "Move in the direction of courage and rise to the occasion. … There are seasons and cycles to every creative process."

Move in the direction of courage and rise to the occasion. This idea that everything that comes in is just supposed to be effortless and in flow is not the whole story. It's just not, and it stops more good projects, things that we need to be creating. There are seasons and cycles to every creative process.

So, Claire and I are in a bricklaying process right now and it's taken the best of both of us, and yet because of it, I'm confident that the work *will* realise its potential in the world and the seeds that have been planted are going to be fruitful. I just want to encourage all of us to learn that; men know this. Men know how to dig ditches, and we're learning how to dig ditches, too.

Thanks for sharing that, Katherine. That's a really important point; this perseverance and determination and not giving up too soon and seeing it as a sign.

So what were the key outcomes you wanted from the Feminine Power course?

When Claire and I first met seven years ago, we actually created a mission statement. I had my *Calling in "The One"* workshop students and we could only take thirty people in the classroom. So all together just a few hundred students had completed their training by 2005.

But we both felt the potential of our connection that we had with each other; we both felt what the future possibilities were, and actually took a stand to empower, to inspire and catalyse not just a few hundred women, but *millions* of Western women to begin generating greater levels of goodness, care and wellbeing into our world. That's what we took the stand for and actually created it as a mission statement, typed it up, put it up on the wall and began to relate to each other as partners inside that vision.

Really, everything – what we have created together and bonded over – has come from that. We've been through a lot together; we're like sisters. Anybody who's ever had a sister knows that you go through cycles; you have all sorts of ups and downs with your sister. But the foundation of the connection is such a strong soul bond and there is a commitment to fulfilling the mission together.

I think we've been very, very true to this, and we're still true to it.

That is our original vision, and I don't think we've realised it yet. I don't think we've yet inspired millions of Western women to lead the way towards an empowered future. We've inspired tens of thousands of Western women, but we want to inspire them also by offering the teaching that's going to help them to develop, to become who they (we) need to be in order to really realise these deeper potentials. There's all this potential that's waking up in women and this sense that there's a big destiny that we individually and collectively hold. Yet we don't really have the development collectively to be able to step into the fullness of our game. And so the Feminine Power teachings are the foundational principles of the development that needs to be engaged in order for us to realise the fullness of our potentials in this lifetime.

So that's our particular offering – the developmental pathway that's going to allow women to realise the fullness of their potential and to close the gap between yearnings and the longings that we're sensing about the contributions we're holding and our ability to actually manifest those and live those and bring them home.

> "There's all this potential that's waking up in women and this sense that there's a big destiny that we individually and collectively hold…"

And you and Claire are currently co-writing a book on 'Feminine Power'. Is that to reach a wider audience?

Absolutely. We're hoping to have it out in many languages simultaneously. We have a very big vision for that book. We've been building together to offer these insights to women worldwide and to be able to catalyse the power necessary for a full flourishing of life for ourselves and for our world.

Since you co-created Feminine Power, you also created Conscious Uncoupling. It must have been a really difficult time when you and Mark were splitting, especially having written Calling In "The One". How did you handle that?

Well, I think whenever we're having a really hard time, which is a part of all of us; it's very important to relate to the challenges that are happening in an evolutionary framework. So, number one: it's this deep faith in the overall goodness of life and it's the recognition that challenges, obstacles and setbacks in life are really an opportunity to grow ourselves in ways that we've not been able to do so before. I also just made a decision, from the deepest part of myself, that I was going to make something very beautiful of this.

When life presents us with these deeply disappointing experiences, it's really up to us to respond in ways that are going to bring depth and meaning and turn them into something of merit. It's important to remember that all of us go through these experiences and how we navigate disappointment is going to be the backbone of our existence. It's a really critical skill to develop for all of us.

What message do you have for anyone going through a difficult time in a relationship?

Any of us who are conscious know at this point to examine ourselves and to look at how *we* have been co-creating situations and duplicating old patterns. That's part of being a conscious, awakening person. But there is a tendency to make ourselves wrong if things don't go the way we thought they should go, or we hoped that they would go, or that we had committed to how they will go. There's always an importance of self-examination that's oriented towards development. There's a way to self-examine that is shaming and is actually *not* going to lead to growth, and then there's a way to self-examine that *does* lead to growth and evolution and maturation.

It's important that we know the difference and begin to cultivate the habit of what we call in the Feminine Power and Conscious Uncoupling programmes, 'empowered self-reflection' – how to ask questions of us that really leads to an authentic inquiry into ourselves as Source with humility, and the recognition that we are part of all of humanity that's at this level, developmentally. It's not a personal shame. What we're struggling with, a million other people are struggling with also, at this very moment. This is ours to evolve and to grow. So for instance, where we have failed to love other people, it's not necessarily a personal failure. We could also look at it as an evolutionary edge for all of us and how we need to learn to love one another.

And so, when you are relating to it like that, you can see it authentically, but you are related to it in a way that inspires your own participation in growth and evolution. If you make it a personal shame, it gets stuck and it doesn't really move forward. It doesn't lead to evolution. It's like if you have a thirteen-year old daughter who is overweight and you look at her and say, "Oh, you are so disgusting, fat girl," it doesn't inspire her to grow. It actually makes it worse and she'll probably gain ten pounds.

But if you say to her, "Sweetheart, let's look together at this. First of all, your body is a sacred temple and it's gorgeous, and yet, there's something going on here with food." And then you start to enquire about when she wants to eat, what her feelings are, what can she do differently, how she can learn to love herself more. That's going to inspire evolution in her.

We have to be in that kind of relationship with ourselves. So we're looking at our own areas of growth and we're taking it on and we're relating to it, to the breakdowns of this evolutionary context.

Also, bringing the best of our spirit to whatever challenges we face – this kind of *decision* to midwife greater levels of goodness, greater levels of possibility, through this challenge. Greater levels of maturity and depth. To make the decision to allow our heartache to break our heart open, that's going to give a context and a framing to what we're experiencing. It's going to be very important because you're going to make your choices, based on that intention, on how you are going to navigate whatever situation.

Thank you, Katherine, for explaining that perspective. May you continue to spread your wisdom throughout the world.

You're an angel. Thank you, Jane. It was lovely talking to you.

What a rich conversation, full of wisdom and insights! Although there were many deeply moving moments, there was also that sense of fun. This is a woman in touch with herself, her life and her purpose within it.

What I see in Katherine is her unique combination of skills and experiences, which enabled her to work through her challenges, review the process she followed to overcome them and then, most importantly, to share this with us so we might all benefit from her lessons. This is such a gift.

When Katherine offered her life in service, she was given the means to fulfil her potential in a spectacular way, although for many years she couldn't see this herself and felt as if God had abandoned her. Nevertheless, she persevered and dug deep, so that in hindsight she could see how everything had unfolded perfectly.

I recognise those feelings of confusion and despair, not knowing where to turn, but just day by day taking one step in front of another till I reached a point where I could look back and understand. The problem is when you're travelling through life's thick, freezing fog, it can be scary, disorienting and lonely. But once you say 'yes' to service and start on your journey, your pilgrimage, there's no turning back. That's no longer an option.

Katherine is testament to what can be achieved when we offer ourselves in service, allow our calling and continue steadfastly on our path. She's successful in anyone's book. Yet as she points out, success is dependent on one's own definition.

I remember some years ago sitting in the kitchen of my house near Ludlow with a dear friend, Lea, who remarked on how impressive my career was, to which I replied, "It doesn't impress me. I want to impress *me*." I subsequently understood through the Feminine Power course how my success had been defined by myself and others in terms of the masculine values of status and hierarchy, such as my job title, how much I earned, what car I drove and where I lived. Somehow it felt hollow to me. Yet when I took time out like Katherine and tapped into my feminine values, I allowed my soul's purpose to call me. I felt a pull to write this book and followed it, even though I had no previous experience or clearly defined path. And do I now feel impressed by 'me'? From a place of deep gratitude and humility – yes, I do. I set off on my path, one step at a time, and along the way I discovered I had moved out of the shadows cast by others and let my own light shine.

I'm deeply grateful to Katherine for supporting me in countless ways on my own personal pilgrimage and for being such an inspirational role model. We each have greatness within. She helped me find mine. I wish that for you all.

"Once you say 'yes' to service and start on your journey, your pilgrimage, there's no turning back."

JANE NOBLE KNIGHT

SHELLEY BRIDGMAN

"Once you face up to who you are in life, it's always a lot easier afterwards."

Shelley (Michelle) Bridgman MSc is a sought after keynote speaker and stand-up comic. She is author of *Stand-Up for Your Self*. Shelley is also a UK registered Psychotherapist, Consultant and Speaker on Gender Identity and is currently undertaking doctoral research with Middlesex University into treatment pathways for transgender people. Shelley's interest in counselling was fuelled by her experience working as a Samaritan volunteer, a post she held for seventeen years. For six and a half years Shelley ran a national charity supporting people affected by gender identity issues. Shelley appears regularly on TV and radio for the likes of the BBC and Sky, in her capacity as author, comic and psychotherapist. Shelley lives in Penn, UK, with Mary. They have two daughters and a granddaughter.

www.stand-upforyourself.com
www.michellebridgman.com

A Conversation with
Shelley Bridgman

Silver Stand-Up Star

At six foot and one inch, a good foot taller than me, Shelley Bridgman is not someone you easily miss in a crowd. Unlike some tall people who stoop slightly to disguise their height, Shelley stands tall – and quite rightly so. She favours soft fabrics, often with a print, and mid-calf length, A-line, feminine skirts that flick out slightly as she walks. Her mid-auburn, slightly wavy, below-shoulder-length hair is parted at the side and swept back from her face. A striking presence, I noticed her amongst hundreds of people at a Triumphant Events conference in London. We had mutual friends we chatted with, but somehow never at the same time.

It wasn't until December 2009, a few months later, that we were "thrust together" as Shelley puts it. I had been at a Peter Thomson business mentoring day in Kenilworth, Warwickshire, on the Saturday, so was unable to make Day 1 of the three-day Wealth Dynamics Conference in London. I can remember turning up early on the Sunday morning at a large London hotel and being directed to a huge, windowless basement with a long row of white-clothed tables at the back stacked with folders and a large, raised stage with lectern and screen at the front.

As I grew accustomed to the low lighting and rather claustrophobic space, despite its size, I observed people swarming in and filling up the tables they'd joined the previous day, chatting easily to each other. Talk about feeling surplus to requirements! To make matters worse, I had to wait at the back of the room while everyone else arrived to see whether there was a space for me. After 15–20 minutes, feeling lost and unwanted (a bit dramatic, I know), I was directed to a space at the front next to Shelley. There were others I knew round the rectangular table, so I soon felt at home. Shelley joked that she seemed to have frightened off the guy who'd been there the day before. It turned out later that she hadn't but the event just wasn't for him. I *always* take note of the people I sit next to, as they're often significant in some way. Today was no exception. It was indeed the start of a 'special relationship' and we've been great friends ever since.

At the time, I didn't know Shelley was an experienced public speaker and stand-up comic. When there was an exercise to choose the best one-minute presentation, it was hardly surprising she beat everyone! I was impressed. And have remained so ever since.

Shelley subsequently joined me on the twelve-month mentoring programme I'd missed Day 1 of Wealth Dynamics for. So we saw each other regularly after that, including a few days at a small conference in Alicante, Spain, getting to know each other even better through travelling and sharing a room together…

As I wait for the clock to move to the appointed time, I look forward to hearing Shelley's deep voice and wry sense of humour again. As she says herself, "It's not the most dulcet or feminine tone." Despite that, Shelley's a regular TV commentator on news programmes and on the leap year day of 29 February 2012, she was a guest of Libby Purves on BBC Radio 4's popular programme, Midweek. *On an even lighter note, Shelley recently won Silver Stand-Up of the Year Award for over-55s at the Leicester Comedy Festival.*

Time for our call…

Good morning, Pilgrim Mother.

Good morning, Shelley Bridgman, Star of Radio, TV and Silver Stand-up Comic of the Year. It seems that things are really taking off for you.

[Laughing] Thank you for pumping me up! Feet on the ground though. I'm not sure what's going to happen, but I'm sure something is; you're right.

Now, your story, Shelley, is unusual to say the least because you weren't actually born into a girl's body, were you? You were born a boy.

That was the diagnosis, yes.

Take me back to your early memories. It must have been incredibly difficult and confusing.

Well, you know, the thing is, we're dealt a deck of cards, aren't we? And I think that when we don't know any different, it's not the same as something being imposed on you when you're older and more aware; so I just looked at it that way. I knew nothing else and I never felt hard done by. I did feel *odd* from a very early age, and I knew something was wrong. But because I couldn't put words to it, I just got on with it. I think that's the key issue. I don't really have a story that says, "Oh my God, it was terrible," because when you don't know any different, you don't know any different.

"I did feel 'odd' from a very early age. … But because I couldn't put words to it, I just got on with it."

When did you become aware of feeling 'odd', to use your word?

My first firm recollection was my first day at school. I think it's something to do with the social consequence of who you are because I was growing up in an era when we didn't really have nurseries, so I hadn't mixed in with other children and been faced with the stereotyping. Where I lived children were cared for by either parent while one worked. I think that was the key. It was my suddenly realising I was being treated in a gender that I didn't really associate with, if that makes sense.

Yes. You and I are similar ages. Primary school was very much about stereotypes. I can remember girls wearing trousers was really frowned upon.

I think in those days the genders were very clearly defined. Girls wore skirts and boys wore shorts until they were ten or eleven. Then when they went to senior school, they wore long trousers and that was it. There was never any real question about it. That's just the way it was.

At school, absolutely. Fortunately outside of school, I had more freedom. I was often described as a tomboy, mad on cowboys and 'injuns', wearing a Wild West outfit, riding ponies, getting a gun with caps for Christmas. But that was acceptable somehow, smiled upon even. For me, men and boys just seemed to have more exciting lives on TV.

The thing is, though, when I got to school I was called names like 'sissy' and suchlike. It was quite distressing for a few days. Then I buckled down to complying with the role I was being assigned to because I soon felt that I was going to have a really hard time if I continued trying to play with the girls, and things like that. So I very soon recognised that I had to keep a lid on this and just keep it to myself – I just got on with it.

When did you decide you couldn't conform to people's expectations anymore?

I'm not sure there was a particular time. What happened was the feeling persisted that I should be female. It would come in waves where I'd think about it every minute. Then I could go weeks and months, even, and largely put it to the back of my mind. But it was always there.

I remember doing boxing, which is a very macho thing. They were kitting us out in fancy dressing gowns at a club I joined. I remember picking one that was really conservative instead of a nice satin one in black and gold because I didn't want to give any clues, you know. I thought people might guess. So there I was, getting into a ring trying to beat seven bells out of somebody and I'm worried that somebody might twig that actually, deep down inside, there's this girl lurking.

So was it a conscious thing to do something so extremely masculine?

By that time, I was getting bullied a lot for being skinny and effeminate, so I wised up. It was sink or swim. I lived on a pretty rough council estate even by today's standards. Kids were kids, and it was a bit of a dog-eat-dog world out there really. The school I went to was very sports orientated and that was my escape route. I was good at football and boxing and things like that. That meant I was included. I was one of the gang, as it were.

Then I'd come home from a boxing bout on a Friday night and, if my parents were out, I'd nip upstairs and put my sister's dress on. So it was that kind of duality that was going on all the time.

> "So there I was, getting into a ring trying to beat seven bells out of somebody and I'm worried that somebody might twig that actually, deep down inside, there's this girl lurking."

Were your parents and sister aware of what you were going through?

No, but I remember my mum taking me to the doctor about something and then saying, "By the way, I caught him wearing his sister's dress and I'm really worried he's going to get bullied."

The doctor said, "Oh don't worry, he'll grow out of it." Wrong. Well, I always joke that I did because I'm six foot one. We never ever discussed it again.

Yes, you are tall.

But, for a boy I wasn't. Although I was six foot when I was fourteen, so I was then. Thank God I stopped. I only grew about another inch. But, of course, for boys, it was nothing unusual.

So what did you go into when you left school?

I was a barrister's clerk in the Temple. My cousin was one already. It's one of those jobs that weren't advertised. You had to know somebody and then you would go for an interview when you were alerted that there was a post.

I couldn't wait to leave school. I got dispensation to leave at Easter, a month before my fifteenth birthday. I hated school the first day I went there and I hated it when I left. I didn't have a single GCE or anything.

How long did you work as a barrister's clerk?

I got a bit fed up after a year with the, "Yes sir, no sir." I thought it was a very servile job. In those days it was. Though, barrister's clerks, by the way, make more money than the barrister. There's nothing servile about the job in a sense, but it wasn't really for me.

A friend of mine worked for a bookmaker. By then I was very interested in clothes, and Carnaby Street was just coming on the scene. I heard about a credit bookmaker, not a shop. They were looking for people in the accounts department. I remember I went from earning five pounds a week as a barrister's clerk to nine pounds a week with tons of overtime. So at the age of sixteen, in 1963, when the average annual wage in the country was £1,000, I was earning far more than that; I was like a kid in a sweetshop buying clothes in Carnaby Street and partying all the time.

And were you able to indulge in the more feminine influences that were coming into menswear fashions in the '60s?

They were still masculine, so what I did was shop at a store which you will remember, called C&A, that had a policy where if you bought something, you could take it back within a month and get a full refund. So I would buy clothes for my 'girlfriend', take them home and leave the label in and I would very carefully wear them a couple of times and make sure they didn't get soiled or anything. Then I would take them back.

I had a strategy so people didn't cotton onto the fact they might be for me. They probably knew anyway, didn't they? …

"How big is your girlfriend?"

"Oh, she's about the same size as me."

I'd rotate the branches – Marble Arch, Bond Street, Oxford Circus, Kensington – so I would never visit the same store within a month or six weeks. It worked quite well for about two or three years.

Did you get found out?

No, it was very secretive. I lived with my parents, but I'd dress up when they were out. My dad was working and there would always be an opportunity. I used to hide it all in a suitcase in the loft. So I lived in a twilight world, really, of cross-dressing in secret for years.

It was always more than the clothes though. But again, I would just try and suppress it and suppress it. I would get girlfriends really easily. They liked me because I used to comment on their makeup and clothes. I was a Mod, interested in fashion, so girls were attracted to me. I always had the most up-to-date clothes because I was earning a lot of money. The boys' clothes I would buy in John Stephen's in Carnaby Street, but I was quite conservative for a Mod. I didn't want to give a clue that people might have thought I was a bit girly, so I used to try and hide it. There would have been boys who would have worn more flamboyant clothes than me, but I was careful not to make anyone suspicious.

What happened next?

I got married. Then I think the identity just intensified and, ultimately, I just couldn't hack it anymore. I got really ill. I was drinking alcohol 'for England', and eventually I had a breakdown. I just had to confront it. I couldn't live a lie anymore.

I was very lucky because I had a supportive family. My partner, the woman I married who was heterosexual, remarkably worked through it with me. It's quite simple really. Once you face up to who you are in life, it's always a lot easier afterwards.

It must have been a huge benefit for you that your family stayed together and there was so much support.

I think it was literally life and death in those days. I also had an amazing, supportive friend, Valerie, who's in the book I'm writing.

Staying together with my partner wasn't an overnight decision because the assumption was that we would part. When she found out about it and we discussed it, I was still having treatment and trying to see if I could find a way of not actually transitioning although, deep down, I always knew that's what I needed to do.

Once that was decided, because the children were young, we agreed we would stay together and do our best to bring the children up as best we could. We reasoned that the love of two parents was better than one, even if one parent was a bit bizarre. What we realised, after a while, is that we were best friends. So, whilst we're not in a conventional marriage, we're very close. We holiday together. We spend time with the children together, although they're grown women now and, with my granddaughter, I'm a granny now.

It was something that evolved really. People will often say, "How did that happen? How did you stay together?" Well, on day one, we didn't know we would. I was prepared to live on my own if I had to because that's the bottom line. I always say to people, "If you're not prepared for that,

> "We reasoned that the love of two parents was better than one, even if one parent was a bit bizarre."

think very carefully about it. Only do this if you really feel that it's something that you have to do because you can lose a lot." Luckily for me, I didn't. I lost a lot of friends, but then I got better ones, like you, afterwards. And with my family, Mum and one sister were fine. Dad and one sister weren't … 50/50. Not bad odds.

And how did your children react?

Well, you know, children, when they're young, they are very, very bright and adaptable. What they want is to be loved and feel safe. If you can give them those two things, that's what they want. I think it would have been more difficult had they been teenagers. But they were great. We didn't force it on them. We decided that I wouldn't be involved in the conversation; their mum would explain what was happening. They were about six and three at the time. And, by the way, nobody should have children if they know they're going to do this because it's extremely selfish. I still thought I could suppress it.

> "… children … are very, very bright and adaptable. What they want is to be loved and feel safe."

Years later, when they were grown up, they both said the thing that made it possible for them was the fact that they had some kind of choice because I *was* going to move out but they wanted me to stay. A lot of people ask, "Yes, but how can young children make a choice like that?" Well, they're not stupid and, at any time, I would have moved out. But I didn't and we're still very close. I see them all the time, both of them. And I still, in some sense, play the role of father. I'm the one they'll come to when, for instance, they want to buy a property.

Can you come with me and look at it? What do you think? What do I do about this for my tax return? All that sort of stuff. And then Mum chips in with making clothes. I do babysitting as well, but she does more of it.

In a sense, we're still a family. I feel I was a bit of a failure as a father, but hopefully as a parent I didn't do so badly.

Well, your children are both doing extremely well. They're obviously well balanced.

I think they are. They've both got degrees. They're intelligent, young women and I'm proud of both of them because they both have done extremely well in their careers. They've been amazing. Having their love has been a phenomenal bonus.

However, my change of gender caused changes on the work front. I was thirty-four when my partner found out, but it took me about six years to fully transition. I started taking hormones a couple of years later. I kept deferring it because I was afraid I would lose my business and, in fact, I did.

At the end of the '80s there came a day when I put all my old clothes in a black bin bag and dropped them off at a charity shop on the way to the office. And that was it. I mean it really was. I never looked back from day one. Of course, I'd been spending time at weekends in a female role and so on because you have to make some adjustments. The week before, I got all the staff in at work and said, "There's something you need to know," and then on the Monday, that was it. Free at last.

That's brilliant. And is that how it felt?

Yes, it was just amazing. I remember being really scared pulling up in the car park. Thick snow in the February and just suddenly feeling like a concrete block that had been sitting on my shoulders for however many years had gone. It was just a great relief.

However, in the '80s, what I did was not very popular and eventually all my clients left and the business went bankrupt. So I started a new career.

That was all right because I needed something new anyway. So I was able to start it as me, a female, rather than living a lie. I went for a job interview and I was Shelley or Michelle from then on.

And what was the new career path you took?

I was virtually bankrupt so I thought, "I know what I'll do. I'll get a job that doesn't pay a salary and only pays commission." (I'm not very bright really.) I went into selling financial services. Somebody had said to me, "If you work hard, you can make money doing that." So that's what I did.

I started right in the middle of the recession. It's quite interesting because the guy who was training us got us to make a list of all our friends and family. Mine was quite short because they hadn't really taken too well to my transition, so I just cold-called. I made a good living from it for about eight or nine years. I built it up and eventually I started my IFA (Independent Financial Advisor) practice and employed some people.

I grew a lot from that. I got my confidence back. So it was a good, new life really. In the end, though, I got really bored and all the compliance and regulations came in. I hated the fact you'd sell a policy for fifteen pounds a month and it would take you two days to do the reports. So I eventually moved on.

What did you move on to, Shelley?

I was learning to be a counsellor during that time in parallel. I got a masters degree in psychotherapy and became a psychotherapist, which I still do, working from home. It was a gradual takeover till I felt I could earn a living from it. I then sold the IFA practice, which tided me over till I was a full-time therapist.

I left school at fifteen without any exams and, at the age of fifty-seven, I got a masters. And I'm doing a doctorate at the moment. Fitting it in is quite difficult but it will get done.

Although these things in life hit us between the eyes, and what I did, of course, was quite dramatic in a sense, we make or break ourselves in the process.

"I also have to be very careful that I don't impose my own experiences on a situation ... So I work very hard at taking 'self' out of the equation..."

And you're now able to help others who have got gender issues and problems.

When I became a therapist, I didn't work with that issue at all for many years because it just felt too close to home really, and I wanted to forget about it and not be defined by it. But I think that as I became more comfortable in my own skin and more grounded, it was obvious there was a big niche out there that people just weren't filling. I became a bit of an expert, I suppose, because I knew a lot about it anyway.

Actually, living with something like that and working with other people is a bit of a two-edged sword because, although it gives me a deep understanding, I also have to be very careful that I don't impose my own experiences on a situation and make assumptions for other people. So I work very hard at taking 'self' out of the equation and trying to meet the other person in a very real sense, without me making all sorts of false assumptions. What is really rewarding is how many children I am seeing at the moment who I am able to help. I so admire their parents. Many of them sell their homes to fund their children's medical treatment. That's not for my fees, I hasten to add!

And as well as being a psychotherapist, you're also a stand-up comic. How did you get into that?

That's quite interesting. You see, one of the wonderful things about becoming who you really are is that you start to own your gifts. As a child, I was a good mimic, but I lost that. I was the kid that was always putting a curtain across the clothesline and charging people a penny to come in for a show.

Comedy just got put aside somehow, but my big challenge when I transitioned was my voice because I had a very masculine voice. When I was in life assurance, I wanted to work with small businesses because I'd run one. The manager said, "You've got to get out there and do presentations," to which I replied, "But I can't do public speaking." So they enrolled me in a toastmasters club. I'd been there about six months when I entered a humorous speech competition and I got right through to be runner-up in the Great Britain final. One of the judges came up to me and she said, "That was really funny. You should try stand-up comedy."

I thought, *Wow, that's an interesting challenge for a tall tranny who's got a deep voice.*

That's how it started really. I was with Catherine Tate[1], who was the headliner, in a room above a pub in Islington. I did quite well and I got a round of applause at the end. I thought it wasn't too bad so I did it again. I did a really tough club in the city with 300 screaming lager louts. I delivered a five-minute set. Total silence. They didn't even heckle me; they were just so stunned at how bad I was. There was tumbleweed blowing past the stage. I remember coming off feeling totally humiliated – other acts, too, don't talk to you when you die on stage. I scuttled off to the car and I remember closing the door and bursting into tears. I then signed up for a course on how to do stand-up and learn the basics. I got hooked and the rest, as they say, is history.

> "I thought, 'Wow, that's an interesting challenge for a tall tranny who's got a deep voice.'"

Tell me about this award that you won recently.

I saw this advert with an organisation called Silver Comedy at the Leicester Comedy Festival. They wanted to find the Best Stand-up Over 55, so I entered and won it. It's very unflattering for a woman, isn't it? Silver Stand-up of the Year. No, it was nice, actually. And the organisers were quite clever because they recognised that there is a bit of a gap. I think people who are over fifty, all the baby boomers, do feel a bit like the comics are all young and it's for young

---

1   Award-winning English actress, writer and comedian.

people. I've heard that said a lot. I don't know where it will end up, but it helped put me on the map and led to a couple of radio interviews and suchlike.

I like stand-up. It's challenging. For me, it's that immediacy of being on stage with an audience. It's an instant connection – or not – depending on how well you do it. We've all got the possibility of having a really awful time if people don't like it. The ratio gets better the more you do it. You have a lot more good ones than bad ones, but there's still that possibility for a bad one for anyone – even for those on television.

And did you have role models in the stand-up comedy line?

I really love the late American Bill Hicks. He was everything I wasn't. He was brash, anti-establishment, in your face and didn't care about offending people; I think it was a side to me that I struggled to display. I haven't tried to copy him but he inspired me to believe I can have a voice up there. I just do my own thing now. I'm quite political when I'm up there. It doesn't always go down well, but that's what I like doing – so blow it.

You've just finished your autobiography, *Stand-Up for Your Self*.

Yes, I hope the reader will get some insight into their own process through it, if they look at themselves in the mirror a bit. I've had imaginary conversations with eight of my heroes to make sense of the different aspects of my life and my experience. So it's quite fun. I wanted to give the reader something whereby they could reflect a little bit on the different stages of their lives. I want the reader to get something rather than just reading my story. That's my hope, anyway. Gandhi's in there and three comics: Spike Milligan, Groucho Marx and Joan Rivers.

So, who would you like to read your book, Shelley?

I hope it will inspire anybody over twenty-one, but I do think we all seem to catch up with ourselves or meet our crises in middle age, don't we? So, I'm guessing my audience will probably be more likely over thirty-five, but I think younger people will enjoy it as well. I never feel my age anyway. What was it Mae West said? … "You're only as old as the man you're feeling." When people say I'm sixty-three, I kind of look round and go, "Who are you talking to?" As far as I'm concerned, I'm still thirty-five.

I think that's one of the things that older people get angry with because everybody assumes that you're going to be useless. You can't get a job over fifty because you're past it. It's ridiculous, with all that experience people have got, and in business particularly. What are they going to do? Put Alan Sugar and Richard Branson out to grass when they hit fifty-five? Imagine if they were looking for a job in the workplace, they'd probably struggle. How stupid would that be? I've worked for myself, anyway, since I was about twenty-eight, so I've forgotten what it's like to have a job.

Do you think that's the answer; to have more entrepreneurs and flexibility?

I think everything's up for grabs out there at the moment in society, but I think the days of the big corporation and conglomerate employing thousands of people in a big office block are gone, aren't they? All you need now is a laptop and a smartphone and you can work from anywhere.

So what does the future hold for you personally, Shelley, or what would you like it to include?

If somebody was insane enough to give me a chat show, I'd *love* to do that. I really would. That would be an absolute ball. I want to do more radio and TV, perhaps commentating a bit if I can. Two of my ambitions are to get on *Question Time* and *Loose Women*. How's that for polarities?

I can see how you'd fit on *Loose Women*. What would you enjoy about *Question Time*?

Well, the great thing about not being a politician on *Question Time* is you can actually speak the truth. You don't have to toe the party line. That's why it would be so much fun. You can talk about interest rates and foreign policies without having to worry about the Prime Minister or the Leader of the Opposition phoning you up the next day. That's why I could never be in politics. They all become cloned.

Somebody once said to me, "If somebody made a film about you, who would you have playing you?"

I said, "I think that would be Vanessa Redgrave."

She's getting on a bit now, so I'd better move quickly. She's really interesting. I've always been drawn to strong women who are very feminine but have huge power. People like her and Barbra Streisand, I admire. And I suppose that's partly what I like about Joan Rivers – doing it in a man's world. I think women like that have really succeeded in a difficult world. Goldie Hawn is one of the first powerful women in Hollywood. She went from being what everyone thought was a dizzy blonde, in through the back door and, before they realised it, she became this powerful studio executive.

I remember her on *Rowan and Martin's Laugh In*.

We're both old enough to remember that, aren't we?

And then there's my ideal woman. When I was young, I used to go to bed thinking, *I wish I could wake up looking like Jane Fonda,* because I loved her as well. Hanoi Jane. Do you remember? She spoke out against the Vietnam War. I think it's more their strength than just their looks that really makes those women compelling characters.

Talking about strong women … the mentors I had when I studied therapy were women. I still see one of them who has a stunning intellect that leaves me standing. And I had a wonderful tutor, an Israeli woman who had amazing strength, as well as my own therapist. They're women who were very feminine and very powerful. We don't have to compete with the men with our shoulder pads on anymore.

I think it's a great time for women, actually. You don't have to crawl your way up a corporate ladder so much anymore. I think women have always struggled, haven't they? The statistics are still bad for women in the boardroom. But I think you'll find a lot more female entrepreneurs – with laptops – and they're already coming through. That's how women, I think, will do well in business.

> "I used to go to bed thinking, 'I wish I could wake up looking like Jane Fonda'… Hanoi Jane … I think it's more their strength than just their looks that really makes those women compelling characters."

So looking back, how do you view your life?

I suppose meeting amazing people like you has been great on my journey. That wouldn't have happened, nor getting into therapy properly, if I had not been 'crazy', as I saw it. I think that's the richness of life for me. And then there's the places I've travelled to – I've been all over the world – and the people I've met. Those are the things etched on my soul that I'll take with me whenever I part this mortal coil.[2] I'm very privileged. I worked it out the other day; I've visited about seventy countries in total. And I've met some brilliant people, not just from travelling but here at home too. And that, for me, has been the great joy, really.

I had a travel business before my big change. I used to organise overseas conventions on every continent. I used to catch planes like people catch buses, so I was very, very lucky. They called it 'work' but it was crazy. I used to get on the plane and pinch myself, thinking, *My God, someone is paying me to do this.* We'd get invited to places and explore, flying on Concorde all over the place.

Still I loved it – I never went anywhere I didn't like. I always found something in a country that was likeable. Even places that seemed grey and bleak, you would always find some kind of evidence of the human spirit there. I remember going to Peru when it was very, very poor, twenty-five years ago. It was one of those periods when they used to chalk up the prices in shops because inflation was running about 120 per cent per annum. There was all that poverty and then I'd meet somebody who had a light in their eyes.

> "I loved it – I never went anywhere I didn't like. I always found something in a country that was likeable. Even in places that seemed grey and bleak, I would always find some kind of evidence of the human spirit there."

The great thing about travel is it takes you out of yourself. We all become so insular, don't we, in our own countries? And then we go and experience other people, working and doing something that is a bit tough and overcoming the odds. What we talk about as poverty in the UK is just not on the same planet as a lot of places in the Third World. There is some kind of a welfare state for most people in our country, but there are parts of the world where there isn't and people literally die. We don't really know what it's like to have to steal for food. I met people who did.

Women are at the forefront of positive change in a lot of places. There are places in Africa with projects going on with women empowering themselves and standing up. It's going to be so exciting for the next hundred years or so.

As for me, I would love to make a programme about transgender people in different countries. They have a terrible time. There are places where they can only exist by selling their bodies, for example. And that's just not acceptable in the twenty-first century. How do people cope? If they're born on the streets, how do they live with something like that and find a way to express themselves? There are a lot of

---

2   Mortal coil is a poetic term that means the troubles of daily life and the strife and suffering of the world. It is used in the sense of a burden to be carried or abandoned, most famously in the phrase "shuffle[d] off this mortal coil" from Shakespeare's Hamlet. (http://en.wikipedia.org/wiki/Mortal_coil)

countries in the world where transgender people get murdered just because of who they are. That is just totally unacceptable. I think that there would be a lot of interesting stories and journeys on these topics in the third world, Jane. Do you fancy going on a tour with a microphone?

Oh, I'd love to do that. I'll definitely come with you. After all, you're a great champion for diversity, aren't you?

I don't know. I was thrust into it, so it's sink or swim, isn't it?

Well, you've certainly swum, Shelley. It's been really fantastic to learn more about your life. I wasn't aware of all the travelling. It just shows that when you take time out to chat about somebody's life, even someone you know well, there are still surprises.

You'd make a good chat show host, you know. Most of them are so bad because it's all about them and not the guests.

Thank you, I'm very flattered. We could maybe guest on each other's chat shows!

To me, Shelley is a star. Not just in the media, but in life. There's so much about her that dazzles me.

I love her total lack of victimhood. No 'poor me'. As far as she was concerned, she didn't know anything different so she just got on with life. At five she learned a coping strategy and continued to adapt to her situation. She was endlessly inventive and enterprising; that is, until she couldn't hide who she was inside any longer.

As she says, "Once you face up to who you are in life, it's a lot easier." Shelley knew who she was early on but for years felt she had to hide it. Many of us don't know who we are. It can take us a long time to discover our true self, if we succumb to the pressures of conforming to the expectations and wishes of parents, teachers, friends and colleagues. Indeed, if we spend all our time trying to be what others want us to be, we never find ourselves. That can lead to illness and other challenges as life becomes ever more intolerable. For some people that can lead to a breakdown – and often then a rebuilding of a life more in tune with who they are.

Shelley was clear from an early age who she was, but she decided to conform to the male stereotype she was assigned until she couldn't cope with the pressures any longer. The inner and outer conflict became too much.

It took me a while to really feel at one with *myself*. I knew what my roles were – mother, wife, daughter, friend, manager, colleague and so on – but I really didn't know who *I* was. In 1999 a series of physical, emotional and psychological challenges drove me to the verge of a breakdown. It turned out to be a blessing as it forced me to confront my total lack of identity as an individual. I was a mystery to myself. So I started on a long, slow path to unveiling who I really was. It has been a cathartic learning and healing process – one I would not have changed.

To me, Shelley's such a fantastic role model, especially for anyone facing change. In fact that's everyone. Change is a constant. Yet many resist, preferring to try and control life to stay the same, instead of embracing the anticipation of a fresh start every day. Shelley confronted the ultimate change and didn't just survive … she thrived!

Despite all the hardships she had to overcome, Shelley celebrates the many gifts her life has brought her – especially the love and support of her family. In turn, Shelley shares her many gifts with the world – and all with compassion and a wicked, dry sense of humour.

So three cheers for Shelley and all the other brave trailblazers. We need her and others like her to show us anything is possible. Are you pioneering *your* way towards your most authentic life?

"Change is a constant. Yet many resist, preferring to try and control life to stay the same, instead of embracing the anticipation of a fresh start every day."

JANE NOBLE KNIGHT

MARIE LAYWINE

"About ten years ago … I finally let go of the fear of being 'crazy' and allowed myself to open up to the creative process … It was a matter of stepping into the imagination and letting it take over. It was sheer bliss!"

Marie Laywine is an internationally renowned contemporary artist, born in Canada and presently living and painting in the UK. Marie's studio is an old chapel situated in Abbotsbury, a 600-year-old village in South West Dorset where she works and exhibits her paintings. The studio is open to the public all year round. In her painting Marie works from what she calls the 'interior landscape'. As well as the UK and Canada, Marie has lived and worked in: Florence, Italy; Quimper, Brittany, France; the Middle East; and the Himalayas. Her book *In Search of an Image* is based on her experience and work in the Himalayas.

Marie's painting *As I Think, So I Become* graces the cover of the first book in this series *The Inspiring Journeys of Women Entrepreneurs*.

Marie is also a qualified and state registered art therapist who runs regular art therapy workshops from her studio. In this work, her interest lies in personal development leading to the creative process. She has two daughters, both of whom live in Canada.

www.marielaywine.com

A Conversation with
Marie Laywine

Interior Landscape Artist

I first fell in love with Dorset through reading Thomas Hardy's *Far From the Madding Crowd* at the age of thirteen. I loved his atmospheric descriptions of the living landscape and feasted on his other novels throughout my teenage angst years.

However, it was not until January 1999 that I spent any length of time there when I was fulfilling an eight-month training contract in Bournemouth. It can seem glamorous to stay in 4 and 5 star hotels and dine on fine cuisine, but believe me the novelty soon wears thin. And so it was that I was spending lonely winter evenings in a luxury suite overlooking the sea. In May, however, life perked up when I was joined most weeks by a lively group of actors who worked with me for the rest of my time there.

That first evening one of the actors, Margaret, arrived late, having spent seven hours travelling by train. "Where on earth have you come from?" I asked.

"Shropshire," she replied. "But you won't have heard of the village."

"Try me," I suggested.

"Clunbury."

"That's twenty minutes from my house. Do you want to travel back with me?"

It was a deal. I got company and Margaret got a quicker journey home, although a little squashed in my two-seater gold sports car. And so I had company whenever Margaret was travelling on the same days as me. We are still good friends. I was a guest at her wedding to Andy and am honoured to be godmother to their first child, Ellie. Funnily enough, a few years after we met they moved – to Dorset.

It was on one of my visits to see Margaret and family in Dorset around 2003 that I first came across Marie Laywine in her Chapel Studio in Abbotsbury. I have always enjoyed 'mooching round' new places. Abbotsbury is a pretty village with various tourist shops and cafés. I spotted Marie's studio in Back Street and went in. It wasn't at all what I'd expected. This was no tourist gallery. I chatted with Marie about her stunning pictures as I browsed. The image of *"And Something Touched My Heart"* haunted me. I had to buy it. I noticed Marie was doing an Art Therapy Day in a few weeks' time. On impulse, despite the travelling distance involved, I decided to go. It was indeed an insightful day. As well as paints and pencil on paper, I squeezed and coaxed a lump of clay into a shape to match ideas in my head.

Thereafter I remained on Marie's mailing list. Hence, in 2009, Marie mailed me details of her new book *In Search of an Image*. The painting on the cover was my beloved picture, which had 'touched my heart'. Irresistible! I promptly ordered a copy and read it in one sitting. *What a great story*, I thought.

Shortly afterwards, I spent twelve months in transition. I moved from my rented house in Newport, stored my belongings in my parents' garage, and spent some months with my sister and her husband before travelling round the UK in my motorhome with my dogs. By October 2011 my inner guidance was that it was time for me to settle again. And so it was that I moved into a little 'lock-up-and-go' house near my older daughter in Newport, from whence I could still travel at will. Soon after I'd had my revelation that I was to write a book, I decided to draw up a wish list of Pilgrim Mothers to meet. As I was unpacking boxes, I came across Marie's book at the top of one. I took a break and re-read it. Within minutes I realised that Marie was definitely one of my Pilgrim Mothers. Thank you, Universe.

When I go to interview Marie, I stay near Margaret and spend a day chatting and horse-riding with her and Ellie before I travel along frost-tinged, misty morning lanes over the rolling Wessex Downs to reach Marie's studio. I enter and greet the smiling, twinkling-eyed Marie with her silver grey hair cut into a distinctive short, fringed bob. Marie has forewarned me about the cold in the high-ceilinged chapel, so I am wearing warm clothing and Marie is wrapped up in several layers of colourful woolly jumpers and jeans. She has prepared a small square table with chairs opposite each other by a fire. The table is laid out with mugs ready for fresh coffee, which I can smell from the entrance, and pieces of parkin and flapjacks. There are also hot water bottles wrapped in cloth to keep us both warm. We settle into a conversation. Marie speaks slowly and deliberately, reflecting on her words, with an unusual accent – a product of all her travels I would guess. I would not immediately say she was Canadian, but I'm no expert on accents. Come, pull up a chair…

Is it the lot of an artistic, creative person to be in a space like this, coping with the elements, Marie?

[Shaking her head] No. I would say part of the creative process, as I understand it from understanding mine, is that you *create* spaces where you can be at your most *creative*. I've had studios all over the world. In each space different work was done. They were chosen; I didn't choose them. These spaces were introduced to me because I work from the information in my dreams. That means that in my painting I work with what I call the 'interior landscape'; I use images and ideas from my dreams to help me represent visually the mountain ranges and coastal plains inside a person. I also follow the dream. This means the dream

"… part of the creative process … is that you create spaces where you can be at your most creative."

tells me where to place myself in the world and a general location. Within these parameters I find the exact spot where I'm to live and paint.

There is an added bonus; in these locations the dreams are much better. I only realise this after being in the location for some time. It's like a gradual dawning.

I've trusted this process implicitly. That's why under these circumstances I always do as I'm told. The time-span from dreaming about the location, finding it and moving into it is a slow process. It doesn't happen overnight.

I've been in the chapel for twenty years – the longest I've been in any one studio. In this space, I'm consolidating the work from my previous studios and exploring the space where the dream and life meet. The realisation that such a space exists came to me in my studio in the Himalayas.

When you were growing up in Canada, Marie, were you aware of your dreams then? Did you always have this vision of being an artist?

I was aware from the age of seven that I'd be an artist. I had a teacher who introduced me to painting and told me that I had a talent for it. Around the same time, my older sister was showing me a drawing she had done. As I was looking at it, I realised that it would look much better if she made a slight change to one aspect of the drawing. The striking thing here is that I knew I could do a much better job. This experience has never left me. I've always had the ability to 'see' a better way of doing things.

Let me tell you about an experience I had as a three year old. One particular sunny day, I was listening to music on the radio. I started to twirl to the rhythm of the music when suddenly everything in the room became one; I was at one with the music and the music was at one with me. I was the sun; the sun was me. I was the wooden floor; the floor was me. In this process of fusion I was lifted into another space. And just as suddenly as the process began, it finished. I felt myself separating from all of the elements in the room and all the elements separated from me.

This was such an extraordinary experience. As a three year old, I didn't have the words to describe it, but I liked it. I knew I had experienced something significant. When it finished, the real world was very flat. The floor was the floor, the sun was the sun, the music was the music. All the elements separated.

I started to look unsuccessfully for the experience again. Then one day – this could have been two years later because I was a little older – I was out playing in the snow by myself and all of a sudden I heard this sound. It was like a bubble came down and covered me. Within this bubble, there was another child. I don't remember what we talked about or what we did because it seemed like time stood still. And just as suddenly, the bubble lifted, the child disappeared, and I was left in the snow. I realised I didn't ask her name. So I started knocking on all the doors in the neighbourhood to see where this little girl lived. Of course, some of the neighbours got back to my mother because I wouldn't take no for an answer. I had to go in and look. My mother got very cross and said that whatever my imagination was, it couldn't drift into the neighbourhood,

> "My mother got very cross and said that whatever my imagination was … if I continued along this vein, I would go 'crazy'."

and if I continued along this vein, I would go *crazy*.

My mother said the word 'crazy' with such fear that I thought this must be something to avoid at all costs. So I was very, very careful not to continue to look because it was a line I did not want to cross. And so, many years went by as they do when you're a child. There were a couple of experiences along the same line, but I just kept them to myself, although I continued to look without being obvious about it.

It wasn't until my postgraduate training in Art Therapy that I finally discovered what this 'experience' was. And what a revelation it was to find out that it is something within myself. It's an ability to transcend. This opened up a whole new world for me because I didn't have to look any longer. It was not out in the world as I thought but within me – it was mine – and that was a real treasure.

What do you understand now of what was happening to you then?

I was a very precocious child who was born, almost, with an antenna to feel my way around, which must have been very disconcerting for my mother. She would tell me things and I would say, "No, that's not what you mean." I understand now that I was a child who was so aware of my position in the world, making me totally independent from my mother and father. I'm under their care, but I *know* where I'm going. That's very difficult, I think, for a parent. And for the child, the feeling of being misunderstood sets in.

As an adult I had a dream where I became aware of a meeting I had before I was born with what I call 'my elders'. In this dream I laid out what my journey for this lifetime would be. In the dream/ meeting I was asked, "Are you sure? You sometimes take on more than you can manage."

I replied very confidently, "Of course, I'm sure."

I remember I was sitting in a railway station in London, exhausted and hot from transporting heavy paintings for an exhibition. In my exhaustion, I said to myself, "What the hell am I doing here?"

I'd no sooner uttered these words when I felt myself transported by a whirlwind in a downward spiral and distinctly hearing the words, "This is a part of your journey."

The dream/meeting presented itself in its entirety in a flash as though providing me with the information I needed to fill the gap to better understanding of where I was in my life's journey.

With this information, I could now see that I wasn't just taking instructions in total faith and doing what I was told, but this was a journey I had chosen to undertake. *Oh my goodness*, I thought, *this makes more sense now.* My past actions began to make sense. I felt on track. I had come through okay. Everything was going just fine.

So you saw how you yourself had agreed upon your life's path with your 'elders' before you came into the world. Therefore, you were taking responsibility for it, trusting in the process and letting life lead you...

It wasn't life leading me; it was the part of me that understood the initial agreement pointing out to me what's next on our agenda and fully trusting this process even though at times I didn't understand it. To me that made more sense than following a path that's dictated by instincts, feelings, by what you're supposed to do biologically. I think that's one of the biggest, most difficult hurdles –

to be part of it, to not bypass it, but to not let it take over. By following the dream, it makes it much easier to not let life take over. That's the only explanation I can give.

A good example is that of a conductor of a symphony orchestra; he brings in the right instrument at the right time to produce the required sound.

When your mother reacted so strongly, what did you do?

My reaction was to withdraw more into the reality of my inner world. For my mother, I approached her world from her point of view; and for *me* I approached my world from an interior dialogue and aware of the fact that most people didn't understand what I was talking about. I had to find a way where I could communicate to be understood and at the same time not compromise my inner world. That takes a lot of maturity and understanding to be able to do that.

Interestingly enough, my mother died when I was ten. The only real conversation that I had with her was *after* she died. I went to visit her in the hospital. There were only the two of us. I remember thanking her for releasing me. Her death meant that she released me from her story. I became aware of the great gift she had given me. It brought on a lot of anxiety because the mother is the one who keeps the home together, and without her I knew there was danger for me. But it didn't frighten me as much as it would have frightened me to have followed in her footsteps and what I now call a 'Mother's Agenda'. Now I was truly independent – scared but independent.

How fascinating that you had the maturity at ten to see your mother's death as a gift. What happened after she died?

My father, who knew my wishes of wanting a proper education more than anything else in the world, contacted my godparents and they took over. This was a second serious separation within a short period of time – this time from my siblings and from what I knew growing up in this family.

I left one set of problems and stepped into another; my godmother had her own agenda. She didn't have children of her own. She would have preferred a certain type of child. And in so many ways, with the actions I took, I would make it clear that was not going to happen. I also became the person who would fulfil all of her dreams. Education wise I had to be the smartest – for her and her whole family. I didn't like being used as an example for the other children in her family, but on the other hand I had to make the best of this situation – and I did.

And so we managed to get by. I did marry, which is what she wanted. I had children and provided her with the role of grandmother to two children. This pleased her. And then I divorced, which did *not* please her. In the end I think she was very disappointed. This resulted in another serious separation, which saddened me.

The divorce, on the other hand, gave me a second chance and I was determined to use its full potential.

Going back slightly, how did you get into art?

Well, both godparents didn't feel I'd be able to earn my living through making pictures. They were business people and making money was the important thing in life making you an independent person. When it came to further education, my godmother's idea was nursing.

The traditional women's caring role. What was your reaction?

Well, because they were paying for my education, I felt I did not have much choice. Then I realised, probably it would give me more freedom than any other profession, and when I finished, I could then pay my way through Art School – which is what I did.

You were really very aware throughout.

Throughout the whole process, yes. My first family was very, very poor and my second family was very well off. It was a contrast, and out of the two I thought 'having' was definitely better than 'not having'.

My life was a hodgepodge of 'not having' and 'having,' and in the periods of 'having' only a limited amount was 'available'. I felt restricted for most of my life in one form or another … It was about ten years ago when I finally let go of the fear of being 'crazy' and allowed myself to open up to the creative process; to turn the imagination up to full volume and just see what happens. It was a matter of stepping into the imagination and letting it take over. It was sheer bliss!

I was always able to do this through dreams, which happens at an unconscious level. I had to bring the self-confidence that goes with knowing a great deal about the dream space and finding a way to bring it into the conscious level. I discovered I can do this through my painting.

Do you feel that your artwork improved when you let go of that fear or did it just evolve and change?

My feeling is that the letting go of the fear of 'going crazy' would have happened as part of the creative process. And like any process, I think it just evolved. Certainly, the art therapy training opened up a lot for me. For example, the clinical definition of 'crazy' differed greatly from my mother's broader view of the term – that moving into the imagination could lead to becoming 'crazy'. I'm so very grateful for the training because it taught me the words I needed in order to put together everything that I had done up to that point in my life and my painting, and giving it a more defined meaning for me. I find myself working with material from the unconscious at a conscious level and being aware of it as it is happening.

Did your nursing help you with the art therapy study?

No. Nursing was more restrictive because it's down to earth. If something's wrong, you do certain things to fix it whereas with art therapy training you just let it happen. Once again I was in between two spaces – one of 'doing' and one of 'not doing'. I quickly learned to just let things happen because that's what happens in the dream world. You don't fix things or say, "I don't like this so I'm going to change it." It just happens. The influence from the dream space allowed me to make all the necessary changes in my thinking and way of being.

When I use the word 'dream', I mean the dream that happens when one is asleep. I mention this because I don't want to give a special meaning to something that happens on an everyday basis. I like to emphasise that it is a resource available to everyone. The difference is that I use it and a lot of people don't. When I refer to the dream space, I simply mean *the space where the dream happens*.

I'm also grateful for my nursing background because it allowed me to do some very interesting work and see differences in the way of the world. For example, in Canada I was on the second bone marrow transplant team and in the Middle East I set up an oncology unit for people in the desert. It was a very important part of my life where I felt I made some contribution to individual lives and in the world.

Valuable contributions indeed.

So where did you study art?

I studied Basic Art at the Montreal Museum School of Fine Arts, where I studied with Arthur Lismer who was part of The Group of Seven.[1] Recently, there was an exhibition of work by The Group of Seven at the Dulwich Picture Gallery in London.

After my divorce, to get back into the world I decided to do an Art History and Fine Art Studio course at McMaster University in Hamilton, Ontario. I followed this up with attending the Ontario College of Art and Design, a high profile School of Art in Toronto, where I decided to work with the information of my dreams as painting material. I studied for a year with Carmen Ceraceda, a South American artist who worked with dreams.

Take me back before then to when you got married.

I had no intention of marrying. I had decided to be a professional artist, have lots of affairs, no children – a free and easy life. And that's the way it was until I met a certain person. We were good friends for about a five-year period. There was no sexual involvement to get in the way of talking openly.

One day he told me, "You don't have to do this alone."

There was a 'rightness' about this statement, and suddenly a new possibility opened up for me. We became lovers. This led to marriage, which felt right because of his understanding of the position I wanted to take up in the world. And so I married. Overnight the whole situation changed from being friends and lovers to having 'new responsibilities'. I call this the 'Big Seduction'.

> "I had no intention of marrying. I had decided to be a professional artist, have lots of affairs, no children – a free and easy life."

I thought, *Oh my God, I've made a really big mistake.* I should have left then, but you remember the things said by your parents – *"You made your bed. You lie in it."* In the single act of marrying I had lost my independence, my freedom, everything. Then I discovered I was pregnant. I wanted an abortion because I began to feel trapped. My husband was a mathematician at M.I.T. in Boston.[2] Boston is predominantly Roman Catholic. I had no option but to go through with the pregnancy.

To make a very long story short, I have two wonderful daughters from this marriage.

At what point did you feel, 'Enough,' and decide to get divorced?

---

1   Arthur Lismer (1885–1969) was born in Sheffield, England, and emigrated to Toronto, Canada, in 1911. The work of Group of Seven was intended to contribute to the process of giving Canada a distinctive national voice in painting.
2   M.I.T.: Massachusetts Institute of Technology

When both girls were in school full-time, I said to my husband, "Now I'm going to pick up where I left off." He then told me that he had been unfaithful. I told him, "In that case I don't need to discuss my plans with you. You don't belong here. You've broken a contract. I think you should leave right now."

But he couldn't leave his family. This made me very angry and I said, "No, you can't leave your family, but you're prepared to put us all in this position where your heart and your feelings are with another person. You're prepared to commit all of us to a life of hell."

> "I thought, 'I can decide to die here or I can choose life.' Suddenly, and with great clarity, I chose life, got up and left…"

The affair ended because he couldn't leave the marriage. I tried with the marriage for another year but could not take it any further.

"I'm not committed to this anymore, I can't be committed, will never be committed. You have the choice of leaving or I will leave."

He asked, "Will you stay in this house?"

I replied, "Of course not. I would prefer to be in a large city," because art activity is usually based in a large city.

He decided he wasn't going to leave. One afternoon I found myself lying in bed overwhelmed with what felt like an impossible situation. I thought, *I can decide to die here or I can choose life.* Suddenly, and with great clarity, I chose life, got up and left…

Did you take your daughters with you?

No. I had seen divorced women always short of money and holding down jobs to make ends meet. I did not want this for myself or for my daughters. It was a very big decision requiring much reflection on doing what was best. I'd had a whole year to think about it. Leaving them with their father meant that life for them would go on as usual; same school, same friends, same home. They enjoyed a good relationship with their paternal grandparents, aunts, uncles, et cetera. This would not change. These were the factors that affected my decision.

I was thirty-six. I knew I was going into total chaos because when such a decision is made 'all the chickens come home to roost'. Looking back, the separation from my children represented all of the separations I had experienced in my life. I was in this chaos for two years. Had I brought my daughters with me, I could have avoided most of the pain. But there is only one drawback; then my daughters would have stepped into their 'Mother's Agenda'. I was very aware of what this would mean for them.

I saw a psychiatrist for close to a year. At times the psychic pain was too much to bear. This support meant I was able to leave the pain with him while I proceeded to make a new life for myself with studies and new friends.

Gradually, the chaos became more ordered. I finished my Art History and Fine Art Studio course, which I thoroughly enjoyed. I was connecting literature I'd read in the past with paintings I was studying. I found this way of thinking led me to flirt with my imagination. And then to discover I could write! The essays I was handing in came back to me with glowing comments.

Slowly, I recovered and reconnected myself with myself. The interesting thing is that I was able to share my discoveries with my daughters. For example, in art school we spent a week in New York. I brought my oldest daughter with me. At the time she was studying the violin. Her biggest ambition then was to play in Carnegie Hall. So we attended a concert there. She commented that it was not as she had imagined it.

I agreed. "Maybe you'd like to change your mind?"

This type of dialogue was becoming more central in our discussions. I began to relax with the separation and thought to myself, *I'm still contributing*.

When I went to Brittany, my oldest daughter came with me. She attended the local school and managed to be successful in obtaining her Baccalauréat. She moved from an English-speaking background to a French-speaking one. Had I stayed in the marriage I would not have been free to explore these new experiences and, importantly, to expose my daughters to them.

You went through hell for two years but what a gift you gave your daughters.

There were *two* gifts that I gave them:
1. the freedom from their 'Mother's Agenda' and
2. exposure to new experiences.

Have they inherited your intuition, your inner-vision?

Both of my daughters are very private people and I respect that. I will not be able to answer this question for them. I say this because it is often the privacy of women that's ignored. I feel it is a mother's duty to introduce the sensibility of expecting one's privacy to be respected at any age.

I understand.

One of the things I've learnt is that one must not interfere.

That day I decided to leave, I chose life. I just walked out the door and never looked back. To be able to make those decisions and follow through is not easy, but it can and sometimes *must* be done. The alternative would have been to be stuck in a very beautiful but isolated house in the country. The hedge around it was as high as the second storey windows. I tried to make life interesting for myself; there just wasn't enough input. My discoveries were never shared. To this day I wonder why this was so.

I think a lot of women fall into this category of unfulfilled lives. It makes me very sad when I see it. Things will not change without making decisions. In a way I lost everything when my mother died, and I guess one could say there was nothing more to lose. In another way her death was a gift in not being fearful of losing. Losing what? Losing anything. As an example, this space here – I can recreate it anywhere in the world. What I try to get across to the women who come to art therapy is that there is no 'either/or' situation and to not be fearful of making the decisions necessary to get what one wants. It's a matter of taking one step at a time.

You're a great role model for making decisions to get the life you want.

Can we just do a slight rewind and look at your various forays abroad? Because that's been very much part of your life too.

Florence was my first experience of living abroad. At art school I decided it was time for me to broaden my vision. I realised I would be a whole year away, and I would not be available for my daughters. I got around this by thinking, *Actually they could come to visit me in Florence.* I made a successful application for an award to spend my third year in an off-campus study in the art school's studio in Florence accompanied by a tutor. It was a very exciting time for me. My painting flourished in this setting.

And best of all, my daughters visited me in Florence. We also spent some time in Rome. Part of the dream was to be an artist in Paris. This was Florence, but nonetheless the dream was moving closer to its target. When I lived in Brittany, Paris was even closer. Before our return trip to Canada, my daughter and I spent quite a bit of time in Paris.

I ended up in England from the Himalayas because of a family emergency in Canada. The weather in the Himalayas was moving into their monsoon season. That meant it would be impossible to leave the mountain and communication would be impossible for at least a three-month period. John, who accompanied me, suggested England, his home. Communication here would be easy and more direct. Also a flight home would be less complicated if this became a necessity.

You are very much one who's drawn to places – Florence, Brittany, Middle East, Himalayas. What happens so you know where you're being drawn?

The dream draws my attention to these places in a very gentle way. It doesn't happen overnight. For example, with this studio, the dream gave me an image of the room. However, the dream did not say, "It's in Abbotsbury." It took me two years to find this place.

I knew on the morning of the twenty-third of March that today was the day I was going to get my studio. The agent had lost the keys to the front door, so we had to enter from the back door. I was immediately confronted by the three distinctive windows, a large empty space with high ceilings and a wooden floor. I recognised it immediately. Only then did I realise it was a chapel!

Recently, someone was telling me that there's probably a dozen places just like this and I said, "But on that day, it was the first one I'd seen and I took it." So, there it is.

I call this phenomenon a manifestation. I wasn't in a rush. It took time. Lately, things happen a little faster. So, it could have been that *I* wasn't fast and so events slowed down to accommodate me.

I suppose sometimes it's to do with timing. There might be other things shifting to enable the right place or whatever to materialise.

I find that it's best for events to find their own time and place. I just need to be ready when it happens.

And when it happens, you think, *This is it.*

That's right. When I prepared for the Himalayas, it was pretty dicey. I did three treks to find out about the place because (A) I get lost very easily *[Laughing]* – if you've seen a map of the Himalayas, you think, *I'd better get this right.* Then (B) deciding it wasn't a safe place for a woman to travel alone and (C) to find someone to come along, committed to it – which became very, very difficult. And finally, to say, "I'm ready" and

> "I find that it's best for events to find their own time and place. I just need to be ready when it happens."

just do it and follow the leads. The Himalayan part of my journey was the most difficult and I did get there in the end.

Your book *In Search of an Image* recounts your time there. It's a fascinating story. I was interested in the cultural differences you experienced as a Western woman going into a society where men's and women's and children's roles were very different.

Well, first of all was the shock when the Lama told me that only the Lama paints and women are farmers. I was very aware that I wasn't there to change anything. One has to be careful not to. I explained that I was a painter from Canada coming to the Himalayas and if any of the women from the mountain came to Canada, where mostly men are farmers, the women would be allowed to be farmers. So there was no reason why I shouldn't be able to paint. Except that the Lama was very determined that this was *his* patch. And because this was his spiritual patch, and it was wise to not change the way things were done on this mountain, we came to an agreement. I would draw but was not to be seen drawing. That limited me quite a bit, but I agreed. Limitations at times work in one's favour.

The other thing was the children. In a culture on the edge of survival, everybody has to contribute. It's the community that is the life-centre and children begin to work at around two and a half. They mature very, very quickly. There was no school so they could not read, they could not write. I never saw musical instruments or homemade toys. To me, a child's world on this mountain seemed quite stark. Chores were delegated to the children according to age. I assumed that because of the experience down through the generations the chores were assigned appropriately. Once on the chore ladder, as a child matured, the chores were inherited from the children above them because they had moved on to something else. I guess one could call this a promotional ladder. Eventually, girls matured into women. The expectation then was to become a farmer like their mother. A woman was also expected to marry and bear children who then started on the 'chore ladder' and the whole process begins for another generation. What I found most peculiar was that for the whole time I lived on this mountain, women were introduced to me as the wife of … or a sister of … That would help me to locate their position in the family. A woman's social position was identified through her role in the community as a farmer.

> "What I found most peculiar was that for the whole time I lived on this mountain, women were introduced to me as the wife of … or a sister of …"

For example, the woman who lived next door was known as 'Osman's wife' and as 'the farmer who has two cows'.

On the other hand, when the boys matured, they were expected to become porters – the men who carry the necessary equipment for the participants of treks in the mountains. Porters were based in Kathmandu, which was the base for all the activities associated with the mountains. Thus the boys and men experienced another, much larger community and met people from other countries. Their lives were less insular. This position of the male would enhance the status of the woman associated with him. While the men were away working as porters, it was the women and the children who kept the community going.

As time went on, it seemed to me that everything was reduced to roles, leaving no room for individuality with the exception of two people – the lama and the honey farmer – and both were males. A woman did not seem to be recognised for herself.

Recently, I began to understand that the work I did in the Childhood Study Series (the body of work coming out of the Himalayan journey) was very much about my own childhood. It is very painful to me to see my childhood as one similar to the children on the mountain. The drawings began as an exploration of what happens to the dreams, hopes or wishes of these children. I was able to identify with those dreams left by the wayside in order to contribute to the survival of the life of a community. I knew all about thwarted dreams because it was my experience too.

In Search of an Image describes both the journey and the body of work produced while living and drawing in my Himalayan studio.

When I bought your painting 'And Something Touched My Heart', it literally touched my heart.

For me, the touching of the heart brings me back to that experience as a three year old. My heart was touched and that touch changed my life. I felt I had no choice but to look for this experience over and over again. It was the driving force behind everything I've done up to a few years ago. The Art Therapy training made me realise that this experience was the ability to transcend. I stopped looking because I know that it's a part of me. Previous to that revelation, this experience 'happened' only under a certain set of circumstances, so it seemed. I was never sure of when the circumstances would be just 'right'. And when I tried to recreate the circumstances, the experience never 'happened'. Very, very frustrating.

My feeling is that this is not 'unique' to me. I think it's very important to have a strong connection with one's inner world. I would say that it is certainly an asset for getting on with one's life journey and staying on it.

> "I think it's very important to have a strong connection with one's inner world. I would say that it is certainly an asset for getting on with one's life journey and staying on it."

I agree with you. It can be scary, but as soon as you get this moment in your heart, there is no other way to go.

That's right. You just follow it – something I've done since I was a child. I'm finding it much easier now that I have a better grasp of the nature of my journey. It's not about me and my feelings. It's more a question of *"How does this decision fit the bigger picture?"*

I have found that if you follow your heart and your inner guidance, you are shown where your greatest happiness is.

And it's easy, you know. The problem comes when you begin to interfere with it. 'I know better' is the personal ego not allowing the creative ego to say, "Maybe this is a better idea". As an artist, to create an image that will touch another person's heart, the personal ego has to withdraw to allow the creative ego to come forward. When you can do this, everything is so much easier. This is something I can do quite easily by the very nature that I paint every day. I'm also working every day in a creative space. It's very exciting because anything can happen. You're alive and it's just wonderful. I think to trust your own process requires faith beyond. And at times even *beyond* the beyond.

Do you observe differences between men and women in their approach to life or not?

No, I don't. I've reached the understanding that when each is given the chance to approach life on his or her own terms, there is no difference. The 'difference', as we know it, is due to the distorted information we've been given about being male or female. If people are approached as individuals, men and women should be allowed to be what they want to be.

I spend a lot of time in the creative process, where one is androgynous and working with the unconscious. So I've become desensitised to what is male and what is female. My relationship with a male doesn't automatically become sexualised. It becomes a relationship with a person who is male. My everyday relationships with either male or female are the same. I really appreciate that because there is no discomfort due to what is expected from either role, it's easy, it's frank. It's open with no expectations other than sharing what we've come together to share.

Do you find the proportion of women and men drawn to art therapy is pretty evenly balanced?

No. I think women will undertake therapy before men do. That's based only on my experience. When people come along to therapy, my initial question to myself is, "Who is coming to therapy?" I see a person with a name but who is coming? Is it the young child? Is it the soul? Is it the vociferous voice, "*What about me? What about me?*" And slowly the story begins to unfold.

When I invited you to be one of my Pilgrim Mothers, Marie, you wrote, 'My first impression was the woman's movement has begun.'

Yes, I feel very strongly about that. I associate the title, 'Pilgrim Mothers', with the movement of the Pilgrims to the New World in order to find religious freedom.

I see the Pilgrim Mothers as the beginning of a new movement where the feminine is allowed the space to not accept the role of drudgery that's been assigned to her. We look after our husbands, our relationships, our children, our home. It's all pretty mundane and on a daily basis wears you down. What do you think? My feeling is that as a female to be given an alternative would prove quite exciting.

I agree. I think there's something within women that wants to be 'of service'. Too often, this can mean 'of slavery' to others.

That's right. If you saw an advertisement in a magazine or in the newspaper with a job description of housewife/mother, would you take it? Would you even apply?

Not from the job description. But one's emotions get involved.

That's something one has to keep in mind. I would also hope that through the development of The Pilgrim Mothers, and the personal development of the people in the movement, that both males and females can begin to see women as persons rather than as sexualised objects, or through roles that have been handed down often through distorted information.

I absolutely agree with you there, Marie. It would be wonderful for far more equal partnerships and sharing. I hold that vision with you.

I would hope that women can see that there is an alternative, that it isn't the end of the world to be independent for your life. It isn't the end of the world to be responsible for earning your own living, and it's not the end of the world to not be in a relationship, if that's what the path requires, if women can begin to see that there are other ways of doing things, other ways of conducting your life, other ways of taking your place in the world, being content with it and taking responsibility for it.

"You learn to relax with living on the edge."

I find that it's become much easier for me because you learn to relax with your decisions. You learn to relax with your deadlines. You learn to relax with living on the edge. You create your own life, which is certainly much better than being assigned a role.

You can write your own life story instead of following someone else's.

That's right.

What a life story Marie has written for herself! No one could say it was easy. I think Marie must have made one of the hardest choices for any mother when she left her two daughters with their father. As she said, she had time to reflect on what might be best for the family. In a moment of despair and yet clarity she made a decision to choose life. She *knew* that it was the right thing to do.

When I have a decision to make, I experience a noticeable difference between knowing with my rational mind and knowing with my inner wisdom. When I know with my rational mind, I feel rather dense and heavy. When I know with my inner wisdom, I feel light and expanded. Sometimes my inner wisdom presents me with an action to take that is pretty obvious but I might have delayed acting upon, and sometimes the action is a total surprise. I have often asked my inner guidance, 'Are you sure?' The answer is always 'yes'. Like Marie, I accept whatever happens as a consequence – whether it's comfortable or not. Marie was aware that she would go into a time of hell, but she took the first step. As she says, it is one step at a time. There is an expression that the first step is the hardest. In my experience that is not always the case. When I know what to do, the first step can be easy and bring a great rush of relief. Depending on the circumstances, that feeling can continue for some time, but I have found that the later steps can be harder. However, if I retain that vision and desire that compelled me to take that first step, I manage to continue through the challenges. It's worth it. I love the quote by Diane Ackerman, '*I don't want to get to the end of my life and find that I lived just the length of it. I want to have lived the width of it as well.*'

I appreciated Marie's insights into 'Life Before Birth'. Her meeting with her 'elders' where she laid out her journey for this lifetime made perfect sense to her – and to me. From then on Marie would ask the question, "How does this decision fit the bigger picture?" As a qualified regression therapist I have experienced myself and witnessed in others incredible revelations about people, places, and situations from current and past lives. There is always a bigger picture. When our decisions are based on our bigger picture, the path becomes clearer.

When Marie talked about *knowing* so much as a child, I really identified with that. Immediately after my first daughter was born, she was given me to cradle in my arms. As I watched her in wonder, she opened one eye and gazed at me for many long seconds with what felt like total wisdom. It was as if she recognised me and was saying, 'I know you. I know where I am. I'm here.' She then closed her eye and went to sleep. That knowing look has remained with me.

Like Marie, I have two daughters. I was interested to hear what she considered to be her two gifts to her daughters: freedom from her Mother's Agenda and exposure to new experiences. Food for thought. I reflect on what my gifts are to my daughters. Maybe I need to ask them the question too – and other people. Let me also ask you the question. What are *your* gifts to those around you?

"There is always a bigger picture.
When our decisions are based on our bigger picture,
the path becomes clearer."
JANE NOBLE KNIGHT

NIRJALA TAMRAKAR WRIGHT

"It only takes one person to stand tall, to step up and follow their passion to make a difference in the world."

Nirjala Tamrakar Wright was born in Kathmandu, Nepal, starting life as a student and house cleaner for her family. Undeterred by her circumstances, Nirjala dreamed of making a difference in the world but without a clear idea how – until, that is, she discovered her talent for mountain biking. What began as a hobby turned into a professional career when Nirjala won her very first race in Nepal.

A chance meeting with her now husband, Dan, led her to transition from national to international mountain biking. In July 2012 Nirjala became the first Nepalese mountain biker, male or female, to compete in the World Cup Finals. Nirjala retired from professional mountain biking at this pinnacle of success and now pursues a career in painting.

Nirjala and Dan are co-directors of Spirit of Adventure Journeys and live in Fujairah, United Arab Emirates.

www.facebook.com/NirjalaTamrakar

A Conversation with
Nirjala Tamrakar Wright

Mountain Queen

I travelled in search of a Pilgrim Father and found a Pilgrim Mother too! I first met Nirjala in June 2010 when I interviewed her now husband, Dan Wright. That year I had been travelling round the UK recording video interviews with people I was drawn to. I started out with my focus very much on pioneering 'Pilgrim Mothers' and then decided to widen my scope and add some 'Pilgrim Fathers' to the mix. For me these were men who represented the essence of modern pioneers. Dan was definitely a pioneer.

At the time I didn't know him personally, but he was recommended to me by Jane Williams, an extremely talented producer/director who shared my passion for stories. I had met Jane three months earlier at a workshop about filming and editing videos for websites. I always take special note of anyone sitting next to me, so when Jane took the vacant seat beside me, I suspected this meeting was to be of significance. I was right. As has happened many times before and since, I found I had much more in common with Jane than the same first name!

Jane had mentioned Dan several times. He had obviously made a lasting impression a few years earlier when Jane was Producer on a BBC property programme in which his parents' home featured. So much so that she made a point of keeping in touch with this global adventurer, who had overcome significant physical issues from childhood to lead a life decidedly out of the ordinary.

It seemed one of those synchronicities when Jane discovered Dan would be visiting his mother's house in Oxford for a few days to coincide with his brother's wedding. Lo and behold each of us only had one date free, the same one, the day after Dan landed at Heathrow from the United Arab Emirates.

Jane and I pulled up slightly early outside the house in a quiet Oxford suburb. There were ten minutes of apprehension as no one was answering the door. We tried the landline but just heard it ringing unanswered inside. We went through all the possibilities and cursed the fact we didn't have Dan's mobile number. Thankfully, Dan walked round the corner a few minutes later and introduced us to his mother and his fiancée, Nirjala. It seems they had just been on a short shopping trip.

Inside the house Jane set the scene to her liking. The cameras were very much focused on Dan for ninety minutes as he answered my questions. Nirjala sat in the background, listening. My impression was of a petite, beautiful young woman with a gentle yet captivating presence about her.

As we finished the interview, Dan suggested I talk to Nirjala about her amazing story. With some encouragement, Nirjala sat on the large sofa, a tiny figure in contrast, and talked briefly about her life in our remaining twenty minutes. She spoke excellent English but so quietly I had to concentrate on every single word. I vowed I would one day record a longer conversation…

And so I wait for a Skype call one Saturday in March 2012. Nirjala's busy schedule has eased slightly, just temporarily, after some major races in February. She had forewarned me that the electricity supply in Nepal is variable, so she would do her best to call at the prearranged time of 1 pm. I am therefore surprised and delighted to hear the familiar Skype incoming message sound at 12.40 pm announcing that Nirjala is ready to answer my questions. She obligingly sits very close to the mic so I can hear her soft voice and become engrossed once more in her words…

Hello, Nirjala. I'm really pleased we've been able to connect today. I had my fingers crossed that the electricity supply would behave itself.

First of all, congratulations on being Nepal's Women's National Mountain Bike Cross Country Champion once again. That's quite a mouthful. You've come a long way – in all sorts of ways. Tell me what life was like growing up in Nepal.

I was born in a typical conservative, indigenous Newari family – a tribe from Kathmandu Valley. I am typical Newar tribe. Growing up was not very exciting. I used to do household work in the house and go to school. In the school, we didn't have games. We just used to have inactive competitions like art competitions, essay competitions and science things. I used to take part in all those things and I was good at them, but we didn't have any sports in my school time.

There were four of us in my family: myself, my younger brother, my dad and my mum. In the house, I used to be with my mum most of the time. She had her own work as a ladies' tailor. She sewed ladies' clothes and she used to be busy all the time. I used to do most of the household work, so my life was nothing more than housework and homework. My world was just this much – house and school. I was a very serious person. I used to think about my future; I've wanted to become a great person since I was a child.

When did you get the opportunity to do sport?

After school, I started running – jogging in the morning. Then I started going for yoga. In yoga, I started to feel very fresh; I started to feel energy. I had a bicycle and after yoga I used to go cycling with my friends, and we enjoyed it. Just cycling. I started going a little further away from the house and I really enjoyed it. I would go to my friends' house to ask them to go cycling, and that's how I started loving cycling.

"I've wanted to become a great person since I was a child."

How old were you when you first went on a cycle?

Actually, when I was in school, I learned cycling, and I used to go to school on a bicycle too.

I see. And was your school close by or did you have to cycle a distance to get there?

It is not far. It takes just fifteen minutes to walk, so by cycle it was closer.

How did you move on to racing?

Back then I didn't know that there is a racing sport called mountain biking in Nepal. I didn't know anything about that; I just wanted to cycle. When I was cycling with friends, I was really into it and I wanted to explore places on my bike. One of my friends who was also a cyclist, told me there is a cycle race and that I should participate. So he took me with him to take part in the race. It was a series of three cycle races and I got the highest points among the Nepali and among the female riders.

After that, I got media attention. I was in the newspaper and I felt like, "Oh, I must be somebody." I felt a rise of self-esteem. I didn't feel like I'm nobody anymore. I thought I was someone and I loved that feeling. That's why I continue cycling.

How old were you when you got the highest points in that race, Nirjala?

I was twenty years old.

What was the name of that first race you took part in?

It was called the Action Asia Himalayan Mountain Bike Race Series 2001.

What was the reaction to you in Nepal as a successful woman cyclist?

Do you mean the challenges?

It might be. Did people say, "Good for you!" or did they think it was odd for a girl to be doing this?

I had to really face lots of challenges. I'm still facing some now and some I have already overcome. When I was cycling, many people used to say, "Oh, that girl's crazy, always cycling so far away by herself." I used to hear many kinds of comments, but they were normal comments. The real challenges I had to face, after entering and becoming a serious mountain bike racer, are many.

These are some of the challenges I've had to face during my career. One is financial – it's a very expensive sport. The cost of the racing bike alone is two years' wages for a normal working person in Nepal.

Oh, my goodness. That's a *huge* amount for anyone to find.

Yes. Our wages in Nepal are really less. In Nepal, we get very little allowance from the government for cycling. Just recently, a few weeks back, I got three pounds a day for two days of races in the national team. The rest of the time, I don't get any allowance. Nepal Cycling Association doesn't have a budget to send bikers to participate in international races. They do only the paperwork, the entry for international games, making the International Cycling Union card … these things they do. If we want to participate, if we think we are something, if we want to know our ability, we have to bear all costs ourselves. We have to sponsor ourselves. But in the West it's different. In the West, athletes get all the facilities of physiotherapy, bike parts … everything. In Nepal, it's financially a major problem.

And another challenge I had to face – let's say No. 2 challenge – was learning mechanical skills. There is no particular place to learn these skills in Nepal. Many bike tour companies are there, but bike tour companies don't teach females mechanical skills because they believe that as soon as a girl gets married, a husband would not send her to do such work and the cost of this training will go to waste. So, I have been learning mechanical skills by myself for all these years, little by little, asking questions, looking at YouTube, like that. *[Laughing]*

The No. 3 challenge I had to face was the lack of a coach. I have to play the role of coach and player and prepare by myself by planning all the goals and strategies for proper training. In Nepal, there is no qualified coach for training for the international level.

The No. 4 challenge is a lack of support from male cycling friends. As a girl, when I go out for training, boys always try to flirt with me and get more things out of me because they think I owe them something as they are helping me. I always feel it.

Another challenge, the biggest of all challenges, is boys focussing on my personal issues more than my professional achievements. They spread rumours and make life hard. There was a very serious incident that happened to me. Once, in a multiple day race in Nepal, I had a fight at 5,000 metres altitude with another Nepali rider – a male rider – and he slapped me in front of everybody, and also the organiser was there. I felt very hurt when no punishment was given to him by the organisers. And the organiser who saw it was British. Nepal Cycling Association was also not supportive. During that time, the silence of my friends also hurt me. I overcame it by thinking I'm not quitting mountain biking just because others are giving me a hard time. If I quit, I will quit by my own wishes. Yes, there are many challenges.

"I'm not quitting mountain biking just because others are giving me a hard time. If I quit, I will quit by my own wishes."

How did you overcome your challenges?

I overcame my challenges by having a positive mental attitude. Now rumours don't matter to me. I know what I have to do. I overcome by thinking that if I get the chance to go to the Olympics, I will be the first Nepali mountain biker to go to the Olympics and it would be my life's biggest achievement. I know it is the toughest and biggest sports event in the world. When I say my goal is going to the Olympics, people laugh at me. But I say to myself that I can dream to go to the Olympics and I want to try. If I can't reach there, no problem. But if I don't try, I will always regret it for the rest of my life, thinking I should have at least tried when I was young and strong, when it was the right time. There's a phrase like 'time and tides waits for nobody'.

That's very inspiring. And how did you overcome the financial challenge?

The financial thing is still a problem. I carry on training. We still look for sponsors, but now it's not that much of a problem because my husband supports me financially, even if I don't get sponsors. Before, my father and my brother Nipun used to support me. Nipun even wrote a sponsors proposal for me and lent me money to go to a race. At that time I couldn't afford to go to participate in international races, but I could train in Nepal and race only inside Nepal.

Everything was moving slowly. I thought that by waiting like this for the government to do something for us, nothing will happen, so I made a proposal for sponsorship and started going to look for sponsors. I negotiated with them. Like this I could find some sponsors from many places and I could go to take part in a race in India in 2009. Before 2006, I used to race only inside Nepal, and after 2006 I could afford to go to race internationally.

When I went to India, I had already met Dan. He knew about me for many years, but we hadn't talked with one other. We came across each other in a forest while we were cycling. We crossed each other's path and we talked with each other. At that time, I was training for an international race and I was also very stressed about my bike parts. My bike was old and worn out and I needed good parts to be able to race at an international level. Dan wanted to help me and we started communicating and emailed for a few months. He wanted to hold my hand and help me. He sent me a carbon fibre bike part, a bike frame, and that's how it started. Since that time, I have been racing with my husband's support.

That's lovely. What a special person he is and what a fantastic story. Was Dan working in Nepal when you met?

No, Dan was working in UAE (United Arab Emirates), but he had a flat in Nepal and just came to Nepal for holidays. When I met him in the forest, I was riding down the forest and he was riding up the forest. It was muddy and dirty, so our pace was slow. That's how we stopped and talked.

I love that story. Was he aware of you because he had come to his flat in Nepal and seen you in the newspapers or was it because he had seen you as you were cycling?

Yes, actually Dan had been there in other cycle races that I had participated in, and he knew I was a top mountain biker also. But I never noticed him and we had never talked. We first talked in that forest of Nagarjun in February 2009.

So was Dan a mountain biker as well?

Yes, he is a mountain biker too.

I hadn't realised that. I know he's a real adventurer, but I hadn't realised he was doing mountain bike racing as well. I know you're in Nepal now for this conversation, but do you still live in Nepal? What about Dan's base in the UAE?

Yes, I am still in Nepal because training, and sometimes the races, in the terrain in Nepal, is very nice. So we live for most of the time distantly.

How do you combine your marriage and travelling between continents with your Olympic quest?

We haven't actually. My husband and I haven't had the opportunity to spend a happy married life together because we have been living distant almost all the time for the sake of dedicated training and races for the Olympic bid. My biggest goal has affected our life completely. We have put all family plans and future business plans aside to work and try towards the Olympics for now. I have a board above the desk in our Kathmandu flat and on it is written the words: 'Success doesn't come without commitment'. When it feels really hard living apart or when I am tired and cold and I don't want to get up early, I make myself do it using these words as my personal mantra.

There's a lot of dedication going into this goal.

Do you have any role models yourself, Nirjala?

My inspiration is Rie Katayama, the Japanese Female National Champion and two-times Olympian. She inspires me because she is a friendly athlete who talks to others and is supportive of others.

You've spoken about your friends and other people not supporting you. Is that still the same? Have you gathered a new set of friends around you who do support you or is it still difficult for a woman like yourself?

It's a little bit difficult in the sense that I have changed many groups of friends for training. But all the time something is not well with some cycling friends. It's hard to explain. Some very fast friends don't want to go with a slow rider sometimes. So if I go with one friend, they don't want me to go with other groups, and if I go with a big group, their way of riding is not what I want. Most of the time, now, I go by myself and sometimes I join a group. There are a few groups of cyclists who I can go with.

How many miles or kilometres do you travel in a week as part of your training?

I measure it by time rather than miles. I want to expend all my energy in two hours, so I do exhausting training exercise for two hours, climbing hills and doing the technical, doing laps. I do two hours of training every day.

And how is your training for the Olympics going?

For the Olympics, the Nepal Cycling Association and Nepal Olympic Committee have applied for my wild card entry, and I'm still waiting in Nepal for some formalities to complete. A wild card is the card which is given to some Third World Countries like Nepal and Africa. I cannot qualify by my individual ranking. I have some points, but it is far, far less than the highest-ranking female rider amongst top riders like the French and Canadians. I also cannot have my country's position. The top fifteen countries get the chance to participate in the Olympics. My country is far behind. So I have requested the association to apply for a wild card and so they have applied for it.

I have won the National and became defending champion. I'm training in Nepal now and when I go to UAE, I will train with my friend. His name is Sean. He's a British triathlete and we have been training there since January. When it will be too hot to train in UAE, I'll go to UK to train and participate in UCI races. I might also do the World Cup. I've qualified for it. For this, Dan and I have a sponsor in Canada called Adrianne. She has a group of friends who are helping me too. They are sending me bike parts and energy foods. There is a bike company in the UK. It is called QOROZ. For them, I'm an ambassador too. They are helping me build my new titanium custom-built bike and my bike parts will be from sponsoring friends from Canada. We are making this new bike especially for the Olympics, if it happens.

That's fantastic. So what are people doing to support your application for the wild card, Nirjala?

I think, internally, the Nepal Cycling Association recommended me to UCI and the organisers of the Olympics. That is the Association who can do the recommendation. If I get lots of support from everybody in the media with my results then it can also get the attention of some international media, I think. For more publicity, we are going to write an article for the UK *Single Track* magazine. If we get more media attention, it will be more helpful.

We'll have to see what we can do to get you over here for the Olympics. As well as the cycling and having huge success there, you have also become a bit of a media celebrity in Nepal as well. I gather that you've been on television.

Yes. It is to do with fitness, which I promote. Mountain biking is very good for health. There are many reasons why. It is good exercise to keep you healthy and another thing is if we drive a motorcycle, it needs petrol. So cycling helps reduce the carbon imprint on the environment. There are so many traffic jams and that's why, if you commute by cycle, it is easier. Also, as an athlete, I have a separate identity, my own person, which I want to keep. These are the many reasons I'm doing cycling.

You're a very focussed and ambitious person, Nirjala, who has had to do a lot on her own. How much does it mean to you now you've got the support of your husband and you're getting more sponsors?

It means a lot. Without the support of my husband, I wouldn't have continued. It was too expensive and it was too much mentally. It was hard to cope with everything, so with my husband's mental support and with his financial support, my dream is my husband's dream too. We believe in following our dreams, and then following where our fate takes us. So we are trying to follow our dream, no matter what it takes. And it means a lot to me.

But yes. It has become a lot easier for me. Many years back, the bike parts that I could only see and only dream of owning, I now have. I have lots of nice bike parts. Most of the things which I need, I now have. And it's all because of my husband. I'm very lucky.

> "We believe in following our dreams, and then following where our fate takes us."

He's lucky too. And do you share the same dreams?

Actually, he has his own dream. He wants to fulfil my dream first. After seeing what happens to my dream, and giving it the best try, then he wants to try for his dream. His dream is climbing Mount Everest, and he said he will do it after trying my Olympic dreams.

That's great to hear. Do you find there are women in Nepal now who look up to you and what

you're doing? Are there more female mountain bikers now?

Yes, there are definitely a lot more female mountain bikers than before, and now, as I have been taking part in international races, they also want to do the same thing.

So, you're a real pioneer, aren't you?

Yes, in Nepal, I should say I am the pioneer female mountain biker. I have made many histories, which I am very proud of. The future generation of female Nepali riders will benefit from me because I'm a positive role model for them. They can see me as a lone girl having courage and determination to do things which other girls won't imagine doing by themselves. After reading my stories, they too can start dreaming to do things like me, or much bigger things than me. I believe they will have many more opportunities than me because the Nepal Sports' Council and Cycling Association will hear them and believe in women mountain bikers in Nepal after seeing my struggle and achievements in this field.

> "The future generation of female Nepali riders will benefit from me because I'm a positive role model for them."

That's wonderful. And do they contact you and ask you to coach them or ask for your advice?

No, it doesn't happen much because in Nepal we have lots of male riders and I prefer to go riding with stronger men because I want to chase them. I haven't got the call from other female Nepali girls to coach them, but I have got calls from foreign girls in America to coach them.

Well done. Assuming you get your wild card for the Olympics, what are your plans?

After the Olympics, I am thinking of what I want to do. I have another hobby that is painting and currently I am going to oil painting classes as I want to do more painting. Apart from that, I will look for a job as a mountain bike mechanic. I would like to be a mountain bike mechanic. Or I might also become a fitness trainer. These are my ideas.

You have so many talents, Nirjala. You are certainly a leader. What would be your wish for other women in the world?

I have always wanted to be treated equally and as respectfully as men, in the home, in sport … everywhere. So one wish I have is for the world of women to have this. I want to raise a voice against male-dominated society. *[Laughing]*

Well, you're doing that.

Yes. And it's hard.

What would you say to other women? What would you like to leave as a legacy?

I would say, *"Follow your dreams."*

It only takes one person to stand tall, to step up and follow their passion to make a difference in the world. I think and feel I'm a successful woman – a pioneer woman in mountain biking in

Nepal. I've made many historical achievements and I'm very proud. Being in the public eye through media means I am a positive role model for other women to follow their dreams. I want them to see that they don't have to stay at home doing what their husbands tell them to do and just raise children. They can also follow their own goals.

> "Success is equal to ten per cent experience and ninety per cent attitude."

If everybody did the same, what would we achieve? This answer is, if everybody worked together and did the same, we could achieve anything. As my husband would say, success is equal to ten percent experience and ninety per cent attitude.

What is the difference in attitude towards women between Nepalese men and Dan as a Western husband? I have to say, though, that not all men are as enlightened as Dan, even in the West. Obviously your family supported you before you met Dan. But as well as the financial implications, what else might have been different?

Luckily, my family do support me; but I don't think it would be possible at all if I was married to a Nepali man. They would not want me to spend money for sport and not work – household work – and keep riding and travel alone. They would definitely not like their daughter-in-law doing these things. I can't even think of anybody supporting me as much as Dan has supported me. I have friends, including Nepali friends, and I don't think they would support me this much. They're always a little bit conservative. Once they get married, they hope their wife will do household work, take care of the mother-in-law, father-in-law and house. Nobody would support like this. It is not just letting you do what you want; it takes lots of effort, lots of support and information has to be taken. You have to trust your wife to go and race abroad. It would be impossible if I had married a Nepali.

Well, I'm really pleased that you and Dan met in that forest, Nirjala. That was no chance meeting. It was definitely meant to be.

I find your story so inspiring – not just for the women in Nepal but for women everywhere. Thank you for sharing your story.

Thank you, Jane, and thank you for making me part of your wonderful journey.

Well, many blessings to you, Nirjala. I hope all your dedication pays off with an Olympic wild card. I would love to be there cheering you on. I'm sure you have a successful career waiting for you when you stop competitive mountain biking with all your other many talents. You deserve success, you really do.

Thank you, and fingers crossed.

Postscript April 2013

When the Olympic tickets came on sale in 2012, I made sure the first tickets I bought were for the Women's Mountain Bike race at Hadleigh Farm in Essex. On a scorching hot summer's day in

August, my daughter, Siân, my sister, Wendy, and her husband, Ian, and I went along to cheer on the competitors in the championship race.

Unfortunately, Nirjala was unsuccessful in getting her wild card for the Olympics. However, it gave me a taster of the incredible physical stamina and skill needed to negotiate a mountain bike course. Close up the obstacles were terrifying. It took considerable effort just walking up one of the many hills once – let alone the many occasions they need to be negotiated during the race. My admiration for Nirjala grew even more.

Fortunately, Nirjala had already qualified for the World Cup in Val d'Isère, France in July 2012, becoming the first Nepalese mountain biker, male or female, to achieve this honour. Nirjala decided to end her career on this high note and has now turned her attention to her painting.

I catch up with Nirjala this time in her home in Fujairah as I have asked her to create the cover image for my second book as part of her transition into her painting career. As we discuss and exchange ideas I take the opportunity to ask about her experience in the World Cup...

Tell me about your World Cup experience.

It was amazing. Dan and I spent just over a week in total in the French Alps with the preparation and the race. We arrived at 11 pm in Val d'Isère after travelling for thirty-two hours by bus, plane, plane, bus, train and taxi! The weather was foggy and very wet. The next day we walked the route of the race after meeting some of the race officials we had been corresponding with for the last few months. Everyone was very friendly and very keen to help.

I started by riding the whole course. There were lots of obstacles I had to learn how to navigate and then how to bring them all together. For example, I worked on the first set of downhill zigzags, which run down very steep grass banks in left- and right-turn switchbacks. Then I worked on the rock drop, which leads into a very narrow single track of roots and rocks, and then into a steep right-turn switchback. The drop-off is about two feet but the front wheel can ride mostly on the rock. It was very difficult. I made the drop about six times and also took three falls in practising it. The hard part was to then link it to the switchback.

I also had to master the man-made obstacles in the town section. I had several cuts and bruises on my arms and legs from my falls. I had one bad fall and bruised my collarbone, but luckily no breaks or other injuries to me or the bike! Dan says we're both tough!

Did you get any time off?

Yes, it was good to relax and enjoy the celebrations too after all the hard work. There was a great build-up to the World Cup with a fête and a parade and a rock concert, which was really good fun. There were lots of events going on. It was like a really nice party. Some of the cyclists had amazing tents and live on-board coaches for the big brands. I loved every minute of this fantastic opportunity.

Tell me about the course.

The circuit is five kilometres and the route is twenty-five kilometres. For the women's elite race

I have to do five circuits. I was race number sixty-seven in the Women's Elite category. I wore my national Nepal jersey and shorts. One day there was a huge thunder and lightning storm, but in a gap Dan and I took the cable car up the mountain to view the downhill course and to see the race area from above.

What about the big day?

It was tough but it was great. Dan was supporting me in the mechanic and water pit stop. I had an hour and forty-five minutes to do five laps. It rained heavily the night before and sometimes through the race too. So the course was mud, rocks and tree roots! I had a good race and really enjoyed it. I came fifty-second out of fifty-four. So it was not only a first for a Nepali to ride in a World Cup race but also a good result for my first World Cup race.

Since all that excitement, how is your painting going? Has it been hard to change your lifestyle?

My painting is going well. I do get inspired by looking at other artists' paintings. I have also been doing illustrations for Dan's articles for Nepali magazines. We are looking for opportunities to display my artwork in the UAE. I like to paint in a Nepalese style but not necessarily with Nepalese themes. For example, Dan has always worn a hat from the famous Tilley Company and for his birthday last year I painted a picture of his hat for him!

I have been invited to talk to the female students of the higher technology colleges in the area where I live in Fujairah. I spoke to them on the topic of 'Female Empowerment through Sports'. The girls who are all local Arab Nationals were very surprised that a girl could achieve so much without the support of the men in her country. I explained that by having one man – my husband – support me, and by having a lot of determination to prove to all the *other* men in my country that I could be successful, I was able to achieve my dreams.

> "… by having … my husband … support me, and by having a lot of determination to prove to all the other men in my country that I could be successful, I was able to achieve my dreams."

And do you still cycle?

Since retiring as a professional athlete, I am now cycling for pleasure. I go with my husband at the weekend only for much more relaxed rides but still cross-country in the mountains. I do miss the feeling of self-praise after the race, feeling good about myself. I am also worried people have forgotten me or will forget me soon. Other than that I have passed the feeling of me not being a competitive female mountain biker and National Champion. But it was hard to let go – especially when I didn't compete in the Nepal National Championships for the first time in twelve years this year!

I still get to compete a little by taking part in local running races, which are very well supported by the government here in UAE. Dan and I ran the RAK (Ras Al Khaimah) half-marathon together in February 2013, and in March 2013 I came second in the five-kilometre Fujairah International Road Race, Women's Category. As an example of how well they support these events in the UAE, I won as an amateur 1000aed (about 200 pounds) and a huge trophy, which is more than I have ever won for any race in Nepal at any level!

Are you and Dan able to spend more time together as a married couple now?

We spend more time together and life is so good and varied. I am looking for work in the UAE, either as an adventure guide or with an environmental organisation. Every weekend Dan and I take the bikes or the four-by-four or our canoe and head up the coast to explore the mangroves for photographing birds or to drive or ride into the rocky Wadi canyons to look for plants or archaeological sites. We are thinking about making a guidebook for flora and fauna in this area, which Dan will write and photograph and I will illustrate. We take a lot of friends as groups into the mountains for canyoning or hiking trips, and hopefully in the future we will be able to incorporate these fun trips into our work. For both of us the environment and wildlife is a big part of our lives.

For the last three years we have been setting up a company in Nepal – Spirit of Adventure Journeys. It is aimed at people who want to take very real, off-the-beaten-track adventures, and rather than being a holiday or tour company we will be helping other people to follow their dreams. Some activities we can cater for are mountain biking with me or wildlife and safari expeditions with Dan, and we are both leading long treks and specialist interest tours in Nepal and Tibet, Bhutan, Sikkim and North India.

We plan to return to Nepal in a few years and really get this business up and running. As part of this we want to buy some land and build a small resort as our Base of Operations. The idea is for it to be 'off the grid', which means we will produce our own electricity, water, food and gas with a minimal carbon footprint. Dan has worked with High Ropes Courses and he wants to build tree houses so that all our accommodation is off the ground, which leaves more space below for farming. We would like to grow crops and keep livestock so that we can produce almost all our own needs for group food etcetera. So our groups are likely to be quite small to make this possible, at least in the beginning. There are lots of ways that we can use our cycling knowledge for this company. We can build pedal-powered machines to do most of the mechanical farm jobs and we will use bikes with our groups for most transport except for the really long-range expeditions.

It is nice to think that I will be able to continue my passion for cycling and the outdoors by including it so much in our future business. I have worked for nearly thirteen years almost continuously in this field and thought about little else, so now it is very exciting to have a new focus and new goals, but at the same time to still use the skills I have already learned.

We also want to start a family and raise our children to have an adventurous attitude to life! I will definitely be teaching them to mountain bike from a young age and I know Dan wants them to grow up in the outdoors with a good background in environmentalism.

> "But the feeling of intense personal satisfaction at reaching the top of a steep hill or standing on the winner's podium is very hard to replace."

So do you miss your racing at all? Or are you enjoying the pleasures of a more restful existence?

It's true I do miss the drive and determination that I had to live with every day, and even the getting up whilst it's dark to train and coming back covered in rain and mud, with fingers so cold I can't feel them. The bumps, cuts, bruises and being so tired I can hardly stand – I don't miss! But the feeling of intense personal satisfaction at reaching the top of a steep hill or standing on the winner's podium is very hard to replace. I know that my life now has new goals and I am going in new directions. I know my husband will still support me and love me no matter what I do, and I know that I can do the same for him.

Most of all I always have, and always will love, mountain biking!

I find Nirjala's story hugely inspirational. From an early age, Nirjala thought about her future and had this idea that she wanted to be 'a great person'. There were no obvious means whereby she would achieve this. There was no sport in her school. There was no physical competition. She came from a very poor country. Her life revolved around housework and homework. And yet her dream was to be a great person. It was no more defined than that.

Nirjala left school with her dream alive but dormant within her. Step by step she kindled her vision as she discovered the fire of her passion for cycling. Ironically, Nirjala's dream ignited from something she did every day as she went to school. At the time, she did not recognise it as her means to achieve greatness. Nurturing the seed of her dream in her heart with presence of mind, patience and perseverance finally bore fruit.

How many others have tended their blossoming dreams only to allow them to wither and die by not pursuing them when setbacks arose? When other people's priorities took precedence? When they allowed themselves to be sidetracked? I know I have certainly had lapses when I felt swamped with the routine and the mundane; when I have been overwhelmed by exhaustion, boredom and drudgery. Yet how different I feel when, like Nirjala, I am following my dream. It is as if life thrusts me centre stage. I become the lead actor, a sparkling star, more energised. The action revolves around me, synchronicities occur, people cross my path who can offer ideas, support and assistance, doors open, and I just know this is where I am meant to be. My dream takes on a life of its own. Maybe you have experienced this too.

Nirjala's achievements are all the more remarkable because of her background. I cannot even imagine what it would have been like to grow up in a traditional Nepalese tribe, with its centuries old, maybe even millennia old, expectations of women's roles. I was fortunate enough to grow up in the West, and yet I remember the discrimination, sometimes overt, sometimes more subtle, I have experienced from the '50s and beyond. But this was nothing like the challenges Nirjala had to face daily, and still does. There was no groundswell of a women's movement to open her eyes and awaken her consciousness and encourage her efforts. No legislation. What she did have was a supportive family – and *what* strong support they have given her against the norms of Nepalese society.

Nirjala's cycling pastime took on increasing significance as she explored further afield in all sorts of ways. When she discovered there was a sport called mountain biking and it was suggested she take part, she did it. She didn't back away. At the age of twenty, she grabbed her opportunity to follow the path, which had now opened up for her. She took the challenge, even though she had not experienced competitive sport before – and she won!

This was no half-hearted attempt. This was a full-blown mission she pursued with effort, tenacity and dedication. Nirjala did not just settle for being a National Biking Champion. She had a global dream – the Olympics. So she looked for and found international sponsors. How many people enter and win their first race at twenty without any previous experience of sport and aim for the Olympics?

In February 2009 synchronicity played its part, when she met her husband-to-be, Dan, when out training. They might not have stopped to chat had their paths not crossed, literally, in that forest. They might have been travelling in the same direction and never met. The path might have been easy to navigate. There are so many variables that could have worked against that meeting. Yet it has been my experience, just as happened here with Nirjala and Dan, that when you follow your calling, life conspires to bring you all you need to succeed in truly magical ways.

The two of them support each other in pursuit of their mutual dreams. Surely this is what life and relationships are all about – each being true to themselves, yet supporting each other in their quest. They have accepted the temporary hardship of living apart for much of the time in the pursuit of a dream.

When I first met them, did I think they were a lovely couple? Yes, indeed. Did I have any inkling of the amazing stories they shared? Not at all. How many more uplifting stories will they share in the future? I for one can't wait. What a fabulous couple they are. They truly deserve each other.

"When you follow your calling, life conspires to bring you all you need to succeed in truly magical ways."

JANE NOBLE KNIGHT

SUKI
KAUR-COSIER

" I always had a 'follow me' attitude rather than following others. **"**

Suki Kaur-Cosier was born in Punjab, India, before moving to the UK where she spent most of her life. Suki has three sons and one granddaughter. She met her Canadian husband, Chris, while she was on holiday in Cuba. She now lives in London, Ontario, in Canada where she combines her love of cooking, people and diversity in her company, Cooking Matters. In 2012 Suki was thrilled to partner with Soup Sisters in support of Women's Community House. Under Suki's guidance groups of people do what they love and value: buy local, meet people from varied backgrounds and interests, and bridge the gap by cooking, eating and learning together.

www.cookingmatters.ca

A Conversation with
Suki Kaur-Cosier

Cooking Sitara[1]

The first time I met Suki in 2003 I felt I could trust her implicitly. I had been working as Head of Learning and Development at The Law Society for just over a year. I had started on an interim basis in March 2002 while they recruited someone permanent. For various reasons this didn't happen, and after nine months I was asked if I would consider taking the permanent role. I decided I would. So after a selection procedure, I took on the role. At the time, it suited me and I seemed to be making some progress, so I agreed to work full-time over four days. Nevertheless, it was a 100-mile plus round trip along mainly winding country roads – a minimum daily journey of two-and-a-half hours. It was a time of extensive commuter travelling and very long days.

On top of this, it was also a time of considerable change and turmoil within the organisation as the Society and its roles were being scrutinised by Sir David Clementi as part of his Review of the Regulation of Legal Services in England and Wales. So it was a challenging time when Suki was appointed as HR (Human Resources) Equality and Diversity Manager. She came on a fact-finding mission to where I was based on the Redditch site, visiting key staff to discuss our perceptions of the working environment – people and places.

In my office I drew up a chair for Suki and she asked for my opinions. I thought momentarily about gradually drip-feeding her information as she was new to the organisation. But as we started chatting, I just knew Suki was a person who would want the whole story, warts and all. So that is what I gave her. I think the openness and trust between us started then.

In professional terms, we were each coming from the same place. In my experience, HR people tend to be rather process- rather than people-driven, whereas to my mind the role of Learning and Development is to challenge individuals and organisations to be the best they can be. So developers, of people and organisations, tend to push out the boundaries of abilities, behaviours and comfort zones.

Suki and I were similar in this respect. Along with our empathy for people, we often challenged them to change. That meant we both ran risks of being unpopular with some – and

---

1   Sitara means star, liberator, and protector in Hindi.

in fact sometimes were. However, that is the consequence of being a catalyst for change. Not everyone wants to change, so they do all in their power to stay the same, regardless of changing circumstances around them. At least Suki and I were able to discuss our challenges openly with each other.

Soon our professional relationship turned into close friendship. Sometimes I would stay over with Suki in her apartment at Ladbroke Hall, a complex of converted houses and outbuildings on a country estate in Warwickshire. At other times she would come and stay at my home in the beautiful Herefordshire countryside near Ludlow. We would share food, stories and confidences.

With Suki you are never far from laughter. She is a joyous, exuberant, feisty soul. She loves life and it loves her. Life is never dull when she is around. When we connect on Skype, her husband Chris comes in to say hello, and once he has left on an errand, she jokes, "He's at my beck and call." In response to this, I catch a distant laugh and shout – "I heard that!" Suki explodes into spontaneous laughing.

When the laughter subsides, I settle down to explore Suki's life, which she shares in her warm, lilting tones, with the characteristic Indian emphasis on certain words and the hint of a question within sentences.

I invite you to eavesdrop…

You and I have been friends for a while, Suki. In this time you've been on quite a journey. Tell me about how it all started.

I was born in India in 1960 and was raised primarily by my grandparents up until the age of seven. I lived on what was then an organic farm; but I guess in those days all farms were organic. I just remember a carefree childhood full of laughter and village people coming together. One of the things that stands out now, that didn't back then, was that my grandparents were actually quite forward-thinking for their time. They put their daughters through education when very few at the time did. There was a specific role for women and a specific role for men. My grandparents, however, pushed the boat on that in their community and had my mum and her sister, as well as their brothers, attend school.

Being raised by my grandparents, one of the things that I remember most vividly is the sense of community. You know there's always been a caste system in Sikhism, which is ironic as the faith is all about equality; your position in life was according to your profession. My grandparents were landowners, so they were pretty much at the top of the tree. But I remember when my grandma used to do the cooking with all the villagers and I was encouraged to do whatever I could do. No matter what your caste or your position in life, everybody was working the soil together on the farm. So everybody cooked together and everybody ate together. I think the sense of equality germinated at that time for me. In my life now, I am bringing people together for cooking and eating, just as it was when I was growing up.

When I joined my mum and dad and my two sisters at the age of seven, it was a hard transition. Starting schooling in the UK, starting a new language, all of that, were things that I had to overcome. But, you know, there were some funny stories too. I remember my first day at school. I was in the school canteen and I started eating with my hands as opposed to a knife and fork. I had everybody laughing and then copying me like, "Oh, this is cool." I suppose in some shape or form, I never converted but always had a 'follow me' attitude rather than following others. *[Laughing]*

What a contrast from an organic farm in India for seven years, totally immersed in that culture, and then to Birmingham, the second largest city in England.

That's right. Well, you see, my dad went over first in the early '60s. He was a college professor in India. His family scrimped and saved for him to get an education and to make a life for himself, and so my dad was never going to work the fields. He was in education and that was his life. He was a visiting professor in different parts of India too before he went to the UK, and that's why I think, for sanity, I was left with my grandparents so that I wasn't doing all of that with them.

In those days, my mum had postnatal depression (though people at that time didn't call it that). She had all these changes to deal with in an extended family, not just the fact that she had another girl. Everybody helped out and that's also how I came to be left with my grandparents. I love my parents to bits; I really adore them. They are very encouraging, quite pioneering in their own way, and I think with us girls they always said, "Education, education, education. You stand on your own two feet. You don't rely on a guy."

But I remember growing up when there was still the expectation of an arranged marriage. Then when my sister had a love marriage, they brought in a matchmaker to make it all right. In that day and age, it was a big thing, Jane. It was huge. So, then the pressure was on *me* to have an arranged marriage. But when you don't *know* any different, you don't *expect* anything different. That was always going to be life, and I enjoyed it. I've enjoyed the West and I've enjoyed my Indian culture in tandem.

When I had an arranged marriage, I got to know my husband – who is now my ex – for a year. But we didn't really develop a relationship as such. It was a good marriage to begin with, and then we kind of drifted apart. We had beautiful sons as a result of that marriage – three boys who I love and adore. They've grown up quite sane and sensible and understanding because the legacy that I want to leave my kids (you always want to leave something behind) is to not hold back. Make your own mistakes in life – that's okay. We're here, regardless. And choose who you want to marry or be with. There is no pressure at all. None of that.

"[My parents] always said, 'Education, education, education. You stand on your own two feet. You don't rely on a guy.'"

The divorce was a bit of a taboo to begin with. I think that was about the time that I met you because I had already left the matrimonial home when I moved to Ladbroke, and I was doing all the travelling up north to see the boys and my parents every weekend. It was a difficult time because it's heart-wrenching for any mum to be separated from her children.

That must have been an incredibly tough decision to make. There was obviously something calling you to leave your marital situation.

Well, at some point, you have to be true to yourself. You can't go on pretending that everything is all right for society's sake. He was not a bad bloke; I don't want to say that. We just were not suited for each other and I didn't want to stay in a marriage where I would resent; resent and become very bitter. I didn't want to be one of those women. I was still in my forties, and although my mum and dad are pretty open-minded in many ways, at the time I thought that I would insult the family by getting a divorce. As it so happened, my mum and dad said, "We will stick by any decision you make," and my sister, who's older than I am but smaller in height, gave me the courage to do something about it. She's a fierce little thing. She reminds me of you, Jane, and so I think I knew then it was going to be all right.

When I left the matrimonial home – and this is very much a pride thing – I left with nothing. I didn't take anything from it, and I think one of the reasons for that was to say to myself, "I can do it on my own." It was with the grace of my parents and my sister that I started over again. This is something I want my sons to see – you treat women nicely. Be equal. Don't have an expectation that they are just chained to the kitchen sink, which is how I feel now in the profession I've chosen. I've chained myself to the sink, only this time on my terms and loving it! *[Laughter]*

No, no, it's different. But it's funny how you've come back to the cooking and the nurturing and the mothering. How old were your boys when you left them? How did they react?

I had to support myself, so I moved out of the area for work. I bought my first house with the hope that my youngest would go to the local school, but he failed his 11-plus exam on purpose because he just didn't want to move. [2] And for those sorts of reasons, I didn't want to disrupt him. Their father and I were always loving to our boys, regardless. We might have fallen out of love with each other, but we loved our children dearly. That was the security that I wanted to give the kids at the time. I didn't want to uproot them from where they were already secure, emotionally and financially. They were with loving grandparents, their extended family, on my ex-husband's side. They were all very, very supportive and the kids were very close to everybody.

So, I didn't want to unsettle all of that either, so I made the sacrifice. I think that's one of the things that you do. This is the lot of women in general. We sacrifice. It's part of us – I don't know whether it's genetic or anything like that – but it's for the greater good; we put ourselves last. I remember my mum saying that when she lived in India, times were hard and she would go without food so that the kids could have food. It's things like that. It's in our nature. It's something that is just there.

> "This is the lot of women in general. We sacrifice ... for the greater good and put ourselves last ... [My mum] would go without food so that the kids could have food."

---

2   The 11-plus examination is used as a voluntary entrance test to a specific group of schools in some English counties and boroughs.

So, in terms of age, the twins were teenagers – a very difficult time for them – but Chetan was only ten. And I made sure I attended every one of Chetan's rugby games. That was important to me.

Were you able to maintain that close relationship with your sons?

Yes, and I am very glad to say that they share anything and everything with me. There is that closeness, and I'm very thankful for that. But they also see me as a strong woman and a fun mum and a serious mum. I'm their friend, but I'm their mother first.

I can just picture it now; but it must have been hard for everyone in the midst of all that change. How did you navigate through those times, Suki?

Something primeval I think – a desire to make the situation work out for all concerned. I had taken the biggest step in my life. Now I had to carry it out, which was an even bigger step. I *could* not and *would* not fail was my mantra. A desire to show others but foremost to myself that I can prevail and overcome. It sounds quite dramatic now, but at that stage in my life I had to prove myself to myself. Having a supportive family to hear all my fears and worries, and help put things in perspective, was reassuring. I also read a ton of self-help books, which helped to an extent; but they did not address the cultural issues I was facing.

> "I 'could' not and 'would' not fail was my mantra."

Also, I felt a great release because it dawned on me that I was doing everything in terms of fetching and carrying. So sometimes, even in that marriage, I was a single parent. I felt like that. We never did things together. It was always me and the boys, me and the boys, me and the boys. And so this way it gave the boys a chance to bond with their dad. There was always that love, but I think kids need their fathers more when they're teenagers-plus. When the kids are younger, it's more mum and when they're older, it's more dad. So he's having the benefit of that and I've had the benefit of when they were younger. I'd like to think the kids are pretty balanced.

And then, of course, there was the other change. It wasn't just the geographical change and the marriage change and all the rest of it; it was a continent change later when I moved to Canada. By this time, the transition was easier because the boys were older and accepted the situation.

How did that come about?

It's really funny. I was still working at The Law Society in Leamington at the time. When it came to family vacation time, my sister said, "Why don't we go somewhere where we're not going to bump into anybody that we know?" Sometimes there's nothing worse than the British abroad when they're together. It brings out the riot. *[Laughter]* We didn't want to go to Spain. We wanted to do something different. So we decided on Cuba. There were lots of reasons why I wanted to go to Cuba. I've always admired Che Guevara and Castro. It's a past history, a transition of history.

And that's where I met Chris, my husband. It's funny because we actually met on stage. You know how they do these goofy things where they mock you and embarrass you and all the rest of it. Well, Chris was there on stage with ice cubes in his mouth, and all his friends, the party that he was with, left him on his own and he had to pick out somebody from the audience.

Now, up until that evening, I'd been quite happy staying with my sister, Dee Dee, reading in our room while the boys did their thing. But this one time, my nephew Dev and Chetan said, "Stop being so boring. Come and watch this show." Of course, we had the front row seat, didn't we? (The worst thing at shows like that.) And then Chris picked me out of the audience to utter absolute nonsense to: how much he adored me, loved me. He had to say all these goofy things to a complete stranger. It was embarrassing for him – and even more embarrassing for me. So, afterwards I just disappeared. Then the next day, he said, "Thanks for being such a sport," and that's how I got to know him. That's how the romance, so to speak, started. Chetan, who'd been playing table tennis with Chris throughout the holiday, said to him, "It's okay if you go out with my mum," because Chris was so athletic and good at sports and all the things that Chetan was into.

Ah, so Chetan had him marked out as a possible partner for you at that stage. But Chris had flown in from Canada and you from the UK. What happened next?

We only actually got to know each other for two days and it was all just very friendly. Then it was my birthday. He wrote me a card and it was something to do with a seedling and how sometimes you can plant a seed to see how it grows. That touched me. I thought, *How nice is that?* And then he came over to the UK and knocked on my door and I thought, *Oh my God.* At first, I got apprehensive and hoped he wasn't one of those bunny boilers ... You know, *Fatal Attraction.* [*Lots of laughter*] But you've met Chris. He's the nicest, the gentlest, one of the most down-to-earth people you can ever hope to meet. So it was that attraction I felt.

> "...he knocked on my door and I thought, Oh my God. ...[I] hoped he wasn't one of those bunny boilers... You know, 'Fatal Attraction.'"

Here was someone who had no superficiality about them. With Chris, what you see is what you get – and that's what attracted me to him ... Not that I was looking. I said I would never get married again. I'm quite independent, I've got my career, I've got my boys. No need to do any of that. And then of course, here I am, married in Canada.

I also remember the pressure because Chris is white Canadian and I'm Indian. Yes, my parents are modern in their thinking; yes they are cosmopolitan. But again, I was apprehensive about introducing Chris, especially me being a divorcee and having this relationship. It's not in Indian custom. I was breaking a lot of ground here, you know. But in the process, I found myself, who I really am and who I want to be, and I also found someone I'm happy with.

So it was really funny because when Chris's mum – a very well read lady who's travelled and understands a lot – heard about me, her only point of reference to Indian culture was what she read in the paper. And it was about honour killings. [*Laughter*] Here's her only son who's involved with an Indian and she knew that my parents didn't know about him. She was quite rightly worried, and she feared that he was going to get chopped up into little pieces and put across the four corners of the world. [*More laughter*]

When my parents met him, especially my dad, they fell in love with him instantly because they saw Chris for what he is. He's just that kind of guy. And then they were mortified when I said about the fears of his mum. [*Even more laughter*] "We don't live in those dark ages, you know," they said. But it's also a reality, Jane, that not many families are as progressive in that way. My heart goes out to potentially hundreds, thousands, millions of women out there who are living a lie, you know. At least I was fortunate, in that sense, that my mum and dad were pretty supportive. But there was the expectation that I couldn't live with Chris 'in sin'. There had to be a contract; a marriage had to take place. So there was that. Chris had asked me to marry him and each time I said no. On the third time, I said yes.

Of course, giving up life in England and coming here to a new country was very risky. But it was almost like I was thinking to myself at the time, *It's better if I go abroad. It's better that I'm not in England because I'm not in anybody's face. I'm not advertising this. I'm not leading anybody astray.* So there were those sorts of thoughts in my head, and that's why I thought maybe … You know how sometimes you want to run away from everything and start again? … Well, it was a little of that too. It was easier for everybody if I just moved.

> "I was breaking a lot of ground here, you know. But in the process, I found myself."

How easy was it for you to emigrate to Canada?

What happened was I did a lot of to-ing and fro-ing. There was no other way. Chris would come over to the UK or I would come over here. All the authorities needed to know was that ours was a genuine relationship. So we had photographs taken of us to show that. I'd heard it could be really difficult and it could take up to three years. So, when I worked at West Midlands Fire Service, I put in my application to move to Canada, thinking it would take ages. But it only took three months because they were assured that this was a genuine relationship. I had even put on the application that my fiancée wanted us to get married before coming to Canada, but I didn't want to do that for the sake of entering a country because that would be for the wrong reasons. It had to be when I wanted to get married – a date that we set.

So, I just had a little mini interview with the immigration officials in London. Then they said, "Yes, you're good to go"… and I'd only just started my job at West Midlands Fire Service!

Well, it's Canada's gain. Listening to your story, you've done a lot of pioneering work, Suki. You've lived on three different continents and you're now fusing cultures in Canada, particularly with your business, Cooking Matters. Tell me more about that.

As I described earlier, when I was growing up, the notion of justice and equality was pretty high. It was set when I was a youngster; so in my formative years I grew up with those kinds of values. Then I had a fantastic career in HR, organisational training and development. I loved it. I worked for the Metropolitan Boroughs of Bradford and Rochdale. I worked for the Ministry of Defence on a retainer basis to unify all the elements – the army, the navy, the air force and so on. Then I had The Law Society role.

I had a great career that I really enjoyed – all the more because when you're working in equality and diversity, it's often the case that you're not going to become famous or succeed at the top of the ladder because you're always fighting in the corner for the middle guy. It was always a case of chipping away in whatever way I could, in whatever measure, and it was very fulfilling in that sense. However, when I was writing policy papers, I think there came a point for me where it almost became a lie. You see you can't force people into beliefs that they don't have or don't want to change. Earlier on in my career, I was bright-eyed and bushy-tailed, thinking I could change the world, and then learning the realities of how hard it is to push that kind of envelope. But I'd still do whatever I could in my own way. For example, the set-up of the Asian Women's Refuge, the first for Muslim women in Bradford. I did that with other women, and it was a first in the country. I'm still very happy with that. I pushed the envelope.

When you're doing that, you're in the middle. You've got your community, and sometimes the people you think you're fighting for are against you, as well as those that want to oppress you. So you're on this tightrope. It's a fine balance. There was a lot of that, but I've always felt that I wanted to shout for those least able to do so for themselves. My career has always been about that. I've made a lot of friends and I've made a lot of enemies as a consequence of what I've been involved in. But everybody has to learn and do what's right for them. So, that's a journey that I've travelled.

When I came to Canada, the nice thing about here is everybody is a Canadian first and whichever country they're from is secondary. I like that because it puts everybody together. I had a brief stint going back into HR work here, but I was a bit disappointed. You know, having done everything that I'd done and then starting all over again and with other folks' insecurities, I hadn't the patience, Jane. So I decided, "Enough of this. I have taken the risk coming over. New marriage, new house, new *cat*, everything. *[Laughter]* Why stop now? I'm in full flow. Go all the way. What else can I do?"

So I decided. I've always loved cooking – you know that. And when I won the Amateur Master Chef competition in Cuba a couple of years ago, that convinced me. This is what I need to do. So now that I'm in control of my own business, I don't need to seek approval for what I want to do, Jane, and that's what's so liberating. Through the cuisines, through simple things like eating together, I'm bridging the cultural gap. When I'm introducing Mexican cuisine or Indian cuisine or French or Thai, I always talk about the historical background of that country, of that cuisine, so people are more informed.

> "Through the cuisines, through simple things like eating together, I'm bridging the cultural gap."

In my own little way, I'm still doing diversity and putting all of it together. That's what I love – people coming together from all walks of life. They've been great. It's funny because when people come in, they're always apprehensive and I tell them, "Look, this is a kitchen where you make mistakes, and it's okay to do that." I combine all the different elements into a package, and a cooking session is great to do all of that. They've been (touch wood) pretty successful, and I love that because it is liberating being in control of what I want to do. I can still have equality dimensions built in. I have folk who I employ from the local mental health institutions who would find it very difficult to get a job elsewhere. And so in every way I can, I support diversity and celebrate it.

You've just been asked to get involved with Soup Sisters as well, haven't you?

Gosh Jane, that's something I'm really looking forward to. Oh my God, when I got the call from Sharon Hapton, who is the founder of Soup Sisters and she asked, "Would you consider collaborating because we would like to have you as our culinary partner?" you could have lifted my jaw off the ground.

I said, "Yes! That would be fabulous." What better endorsement can I get? Someone must have recommended me because it is not like I am a professional chef who has gone to culinary school.

With Soup Sisters, the idea is we have people who come together once a month and we make hundreds of litres of soup – all sorts of soups – that are distributed to the local women's shelters. The London community has two shelters here and they're providing to the homeless because soup does make you feel warm and nourished. It's just to say that somebody cares. It's just that. It's a great concept and I'm really thrilled to be part of that and am really looking forward to it. My work has gone almost full circle from what I was doing with the Women's Refuge twenty-five-odd years ago. But it's all in a more nourishing way.

Exciting times. Well done. When you look back on your life, Suki, is there a message you would like to share with anyone who has not yet reached their point of happiness, harmony and balance?

Well, I always think that as women we are stronger than we think we are. Accept who you are, don't gloss over matters and don't over-analyse; be positive and keep a sense of humour. The more you share and learn to trust others, the closer you will be to arriving at your own happiness. And also, when we feel that we have nowhere to turn to, some of us turn to faith while others have the privilege of having a close circle of friends. Amongst them could be members of the family or someone we can talk to. In my case, and I hope I'm not putting you on the spot, Jane, but you were that for me.

I thought, *Gosh, here's a woman who knows so much. What can I learn from her?* It was definitely that and – I don't know if there are words to describe it, Jane – when you know you're not comfortable with yourself and you want to be somebody else? The people that I had grown up with, worked with, were very, very different. You were very, very different to the normal person on the street. Not only because of your easy nature, easy to talk to, all of that. I've said this before, you have been my inspiration. You really have, Jane. I will say that with my hand on my heart because I think what you did at the time, perhaps without your knowing it, was give me the courage to make the bigger decisions and be comfortable with the person that I am now. Without living a lie, without trying to be a woman who's torn between two cultures, but one that can embrace both of those cultures and say, "This is how it can be, ladies. Don't feel that you have just got to be one or the other. You can create and be who you want to be."

> "Women are great, but I think we can be greater. We can always be greater together."

I often share my stories and build a connection with my class attendees. There is nothing more important than having your attendees feel as if they 'belong', and I try to ease any tensions by being just me. I have a feeling that they now come to hear me babble more than learning to cook!! *[Laughter]*

I'm really touched by your words, Suki. I feel quite emotional. No, I wasn't fully aware at the time. I knew we had lots of good times together. As women and as supporters of each other, we don't always realise how important it is and what a difference each one of us can make.

Absolutely. I mean there is nothing more reassuring than someone afterwards saying to you, like has happened to me, "Suki, thank you so much. You've given me strength" or "I really like what you've done," without sometimes knowing what I've done. They've said, "You've given me courage," and I think that's a good thing.

But by the same token, Jane, unfortunately I have come across some women who want to pull you down too. I always feel like saying, "You are missing out." I am no longer angry, so I just say, "You've got a long way to go. You're living or being promoted by putting other people down. That's not good." Sometimes women can be their own worst enemy. Women come to my sessions. Women are great, but I think we can be greater. We can always be greater together.

We're always works in progress, aren't we, Suki?

That's right. I have a beautiful granddaughter. I'm hoping she is going to stand on her own two feet, be independent, have her own voice, and it's going to be heard. That's the only wish that I have – that she is confident enough to express herself as fully as she wants to. Just that.

I believe your granddaughter is growing up in Paris, so there's yet another international connection there.

Absolutely. Somebody said that ours is an international family, and it is. Here I am. I'm married to a white Canadian. Chris has no children of his own. He has three nephews who are beautiful. Just a small family, whereas you know my family … We're huge. We're big. We're like the Italians. It's on the same sort of par. We're loud, we talk over others. We're very loud and *[whispers]* everybody is so quiet. That's something that I've got to get used to because of how loud I am. *[Loud laughter]*

On a final note, what does the future hold for you?

The only plan I have at the moment is I'm looking at having my own cooking school, and just spreading the word that people will all be welcomed, regardless. This is where the equality is found in my business. If I have a CEO or someone who has a real standing in the community and they come in late, I'll say, "Well, stand in line because there are others before you." There's none of that barging in. Everybody is on a level playing field. I make that clear. "I'm sorry, this class is full, but perhaps you would want to come along to the next one." I don't feel I have to do something or be intimidated just because they are who they are, that they should take prime seating or preference. That doesn't work, not in my business, because I have control.

I would be happy to have Suki in control; for me she would be the essence of benign governance. Suki for Prime Minister! What fun Canada would have! Fairness and justice too. I would definitely want to emigrate.

During my years working in the corporate world, I observed many people who regarded themselves as leaders, but few were. After all, you cannot have a leader without followers. Most people I saw were directors. Directing has its place but not all the time. Suki is primarily a leader. Developing a thick skin is a necessary attribute. Suki learned this early on when other pupils laughed at her for using her hands to eat instead of the customary knife and fork, but then they started following her as if it was a great idea. She used humour and her 'follow me' attitude to pull off any actions she took that were not according to the prevailing norms. This seemed to work successfully throughout her career, as I myself observed.

Suki was never one to take herself too seriously. Her leadership was infectious. She certainly converted me to eating Indian food with my hands. I recall the first time I went for a meal with Suki to an Indian restaurant in Leamington Spa. I saw how she broke her poppadums with her hands and used the pieces to scoop up the pickle and onions. How logical! I had always been a typical Brit before and tried to put the onions and pickle on the sections with a knife, which was always so tricky, and of course the poppadum would break into tiny pieces. So I have followed her lead ever since.

As an entrepreneur Suki is now able to lead even more. In her business she has retained her Indian culture yet infuses it with ideas and recipes from other cultures. There is no better way to learn than by personal experience. Suki's cookery students get far more than cooking lessons. They get life lessons too. She draws diversity and inspiration from everywhere and adds it to the mix – even employing people from mental health institutions who would be hard-pressed to find work elsewhere.

Suki and I were fortunate that both her parents and mine believed in "education, education, education" for their daughters. That was maybe not unusual for a college professor like Suki's dad, but it was extremely unusual in the Indian community, particularly at that time. My dad was also a huge believer in education for me and my sister, which was often against the norm in the '50s and '60s. My father didn't go to a grammar school.[3] He failed his 11-plus like Suki's son, Chetan. However, he had a life-changing moment in his teens when he saw surveyors working outside and using a theodolite.[4] He realised, "That's what I want to do." So, he studied at night class and college till he qualified as a Chartered Surveyor, eventually retiring at sixty from the post of Lancashire County Land Agent. For him, education was an important gateway. Likewise, I encouraged my two daughters in their education. There is a big clue in the fact that most of my career has been spent in the learning and development field as to how highly I rate learning.

---

3   An academically oriented secondary school in Great Britain for which you had to pass the 11-plus or an entrance exam.

4   A precision instrument for measuring angles in the horizontal and vertical planes, mainly used for surveying applications.

However, I rather agree with Winston Churchill when he said, "Personally I'm always ready to learn, although I do not always like being taught." Perhaps if we stay open to learning, there's less need for us to be taught!

"I observed many people who regarded themselves as leaders, but few were. After all, you cannot have a leader without followers."

JANE NOBLE KNIGHT

MICHELLE MANDERS

> " I had a lot to do in this lifetime, so I just did it all! "

Michelle Manders lives in Johannesburg, South Africa. She is the Founder, Owner and Director of Palace of Peace launched on 11.11.11 to assist people on their spiritual paths. Michelle previously founded The Lightweaver in 2001. She works full-time as a Channel, Soul/Life Coach, Medieval Astrologer and Pilgrimage Leader for her own company, *Soul Odyssey*. Michelle travels extensively and her work is recognised and respected internationally. She is a frequent guest on radio stations worldwide and has been featured in South African newspapers, national and international magazines, and on local television. Michelle is mother of four beautiful children. She is married to Sean, an experienced fitness instructor, who also supports Michelle on her pilgrimages and in Palace of Peace.

www.palaceofpeace.net

A Conversation with
Michelle Manders

Palace of Peace Pilgrim

For me Michelle's words are more intoxicating than alcohol. I can't remember now which friend introduced me to Michelle Eloff as she was then, but I *do* remember I was deeply affected by the power of her channellings of the Ascended Masters.[1] They took me into an altered state where I felt woozy and lightheaded, yet grounded and insightful at the same time.

When I learned she was leading a group around Ireland and the UK in October 2007, I booked myself on her day in Stonehenge, Woodhenge and Salisbury.

Unexpectedly – for me at least – it was a strange experience throughout. It started even before I arrived. The itinerary promised a meditation in Stonehenge's inner stone circle, but I knew that could only take place early morning or late evening without other visitors. As we would be meeting at 9.30 am, the standard opening time, I queried it beforehand with the American tour guide who confirmed it was arranged; but on the day it didn't happen and he blamed English Heritage for changing their mind!

In fact it was nearly 10.30 am before Michelle's minibus arrived. Having set out soon after 6 am that morning for the 120-mile cross-country journey from Shropshire and arriving with the first visitors, I was beginning to think I'd got the wrong day. As often happens, those with the furthest distance to travel arrive first. That day was no exception. My friend Maggie, who I had invited along, arrived about 10.15 am with car problems and arranged for roadside assistance at Stonehenge car park.

When Michelle stepped out of the minibus, I recognised her immediately from her website photo with her luxurious, long, thick, black hair. As I walked towards her, I was struck by her stunning blue eyes shining out from her beautiful face. We hugged each other like old friends. She was smaller than I had imagined. I often picture people I admire as bigger than they actually are when I meet them in the flesh. It must be the way I translate my regard for them into a large physical form. I say this at slightly over five foot myself, so in fact most people are taller than me!

---

1   Enlightened Spiritual Beings who lived on Earth and through a series of initiations fulfilled their Dharma (Divine Plan). They now serve as the Teachers of mankind from the Realms of Spirit.

The day proceeded in a slightly surreal fashion, punctuated with delays, disruptions and deletions. A visit to Old Sarum, the mighty Iron Age fort and site of Salisbury's original cathedral, had to be cancelled as there was only time for a visit to the 'new' Cathedral built around 1220. It was a rather fraught afternoon with problems parking and finding a place to have lunch as we were into early afternoon by then. In our following conversation, Michelle described the whole trip as 'very, very odd' before she remembered why, which you will soon discover too.

The highlight of the day for me was definitely Michelle's channelling of her spirit guide Kuthumi at Woodhenge, a misnomer nowadays as it is in fact a gathering of concrete stumps where the wooden posts would have been. It lacks Stonehenge's grandeur, but it has its own understated appeal. Woodhenge to me is the feminine balance to Stonehenge. When spiritual groups gather at ancient sites, I have often observed how other visitors seem to be absent or stay away. It is as if an invisible mantle descends and the place disappears or moves to another dimension. It reminds me of the village in the film *Brigadoon,* which appeared in the third dimension for one day every hundred years from the magical realms.

When I first emailed Michelle asking her if she would be one of my Pilgrim Mothers, her 'Personal Angel' (PA), Sam, wrote to me, "We are currently working through … the channellings [Michelle] did at those places … so it's almost as if your energy has been awakened and called."

It's just as well I have learned not to get overly concerned when delays happen. Michelle and I had several abortive attempts at conversations due to massive thunderstorms in South Africa causing frequent Internet and electricity blackouts. Apparently, the hailstorms were so bad it looked like it had snowed!

As Michelle and I eventually connect, I immerse myself in her warm and welcoming South African tones. There is to be one more interruption during our conversation when Michelle's daughter, one of twins, comes into the room. Michelle firmly sends her off for her shower but afterwards she giggles. "They're so cute. They've been arguing over my tablet. My daughter's written on this piece of paper, 'Can I play games on your iPad?' And then there are two squares with a 'yes' and a 'no'. And now my little boy is upset because he didn't get all his time to play and it's time to shower so they can be ready for dinner just now." Michelle and I share a chuckle together. "How can you be cross when they're so adorable?" she asks. How indeed? And yet her own childhood is in stark contrast to her own children's…

Hello, Michelle. I'm so looking forward to learning more about your life. I'd always thought of you as Wonder Woman, juggling four children and your work. But obviously there's much more to know.

Well, first, I want to thank you so, so much for this opportunity to share my story. It's such an honour and I'm so excited. It's been an incredible journey of self-discovery because so much of the time I was just trying to cope with my children, my work … so much needing my attention. The one aspect of my life that was neglected was in fact *myself.* Eventually, I got to a point where I had to say, "No more."

So where do I start?

At the beginning. Did you always *feel* a particular connection with Spirit, or whatever you wish to call it? Did you have a sense that you had a mission in life?

Well, according to my grandparents, I was born with a membrane over my face, which, according to our cultural tradition, means you're born with second sight. I did display the sort of behaviour that a child of my age couldn't or shouldn't have.

The fact I came here with a purpose was made very loud and clear to me because my biological mother apparently tried to abort me on more than one occasion and I hung in there. I'm told she gave birth to me after an agonising labour, and in my first four months of life she tried to take my life three times. Eventually, at the age of nine months, she abandoned me; she left me in an apartment block and went. The neighbours heard me crying for hours on end. They were trying to locate my biological father and other family because no one could get into the apartment. That was the first nine months of my life!

I was then, I suppose, fortunate that my biological father's sister took me on and adopted me as her own child. She couldn't birth her own children, so she and her husband took me on as their own. I refer to them as my parents.

I think I was about eighteen months old when my biological mother reappeared on the scene under duress. Her mother had forced her to basically come back and take responsibility, but the family had agreed that no one would tell me who she was. My mum says I took one look at her, toddled off to my bedroom, got my favourite blanket and my bottle, then clambered up onto the couch, sat on her lap, looked at her and called her 'Mummy'; it was just that instinctive knowing that she was my mother.

These were the kinds of things I used to apparently do that just blew the family's socks off. Apparently, I would see a lot of things too, like invisible friends. But my childhood, all in all, was extremely traumatic. I don't know what's worse, being adopted into the immediate family or being adopted by so-called strangers. My biological father was around, but he didn't really play any role in my life.

I remember so desperately wanting my real mummy and daddy around because my biological mother had remarried and had another two children. She would disappear for two or five years and then reappear, bringing her new children with her. I remember thinking to myself, *What's so wrong with me that Candy and Christopher get to stay with my mother and I don't?* That's where the belief that I must be really bad or a reject settled itself deeply in my body, on top of the abandonment, which brought on a whole bunch of other issues. That feeling I was not good enough really took root there. Then there was my biological father making promises to come and visit and take me out. I remember waiting, just waiting for him to arrive, and he would never arrive, or he would come really late. There would always be excuses.

> "… I was about eighteen months old when my biological mother reappeared … [I] sat on her lap … and called her 'Mummy'; it was just that instinctive knowing that she was my mother."

These were all things that just weighed down on my self-worth. Then at ten years old, my adoptive mother became severely ill, and that's where my childhood ended. I had to take over running the home. We nearly lost her, but then there were a whole lot of things that occurred after that. She would have emotional breakdowns and end up in sanatoriums, and it was really very scary for me, being so young and trying to cope with your mother who is screaming blue murder because she thinks there are spiders in the dishwashing basin, but it is bubbles and soap suds. Also walking into the bathroom and she's brushing her teeth with her make-up foundation.

So, from a young age I had to learn how to cope with stress that was not age appropriate at all. And then at the age of twelve, I was sexually molested for the first time by a girlfriend's father. And that sexual interference just continued. There were so many levels of violation that went on and it came from so many different angles, so many different areas. It wasn't just the friend's father. It was the shop owner down the street where I had to take my brother to go and play games and he would cop a feel. It was friends of the family's older sons. It was schoolteachers. I would walk home from school and there would be a man pulling over on the side of the road and exposing himself to me.

It just went on and on and on, and because I didn't feel safe enough to share with my parents what was going on, I kept it all to myself, which resulted in immense rebellion. Then eventually, at the age of fifteen, I did try and commit suicide. There were so many different things that were happening to me that I didn't understand. Then just after my seventeenth birthday, I ran away from home and basically survived on the streets of Hillbrow for a while.

Eventually, I met my first husband who I fell absolutely madly in love with and stayed with him almost nine years. That's when I fell pregnant with my first son. I so desperately wanted a baby, so it wasn't an accidental pregnancy. It was something that I really, really wanted. However, it was a very violent marriage. There was physical abuse, emotional abuse, mental abuse … every kind of abuse that you can think of.

But whilst all of this was happening, there were definitely things going on inside of me in terms of just knowing, sensing that there was something beyond this world that I needed to connect with. Throughout all of that time I was aware of presences all the time. I would just simply know things, but I never told anyone what I was sensing or feeling, other than on the odd occasion I would tell my mother. Like the family joke about when I was terrified to go to the downstairs kitchen at night because I believed there was something scary in the lounge that wanted to jump out and pounce on me.

> "… there were definitely things going on inside of me in terms of just knowing, sensing that there was something beyond this world that I needed to connect with."

Another interesting thing that happened, which I'm really aware of starting from about the age of seventeen, was that people would just come up to me and start pouring their heart out to me. I would hear absolutely everything about their life and I would speak back to them, Jane. But what would come out of my mouth … well, I had no idea where it was coming from because it was impossible for me, at that age, to have had that level of wisdom to advise people the way I did. That has got stronger and stronger, and yes, I was like a little therapist without even knowing what I was doing. Also, during that period, there were a lot of very frightening things that happened to me in terms of experiences with discarnate beings, which I like to call my 'field experience'.

When I am helping people, I find there is so much that I understand and can relate to. I can see how all that I experienced has equipped me with the ability to recognise people's trauma and have compassion and understanding when they're in situations like I went through, as opposed to having had just one experience where I could only relate to one kind of trauma.

Whether I am helping people in a workshop environment or just randomly chatting to someone, there is a force, a source of energy that comes through my body, and I cannot even begin to explain what it is or where it comes from. For me, it feels like this compassion just coming from my heart. My heart opens and all I want to do is just share what is there, and what is there is just what comes to me in that moment. It's amazing how many of my life experiences have enabled me to offer advice or make suggestions that people perhaps wouldn't have considered an option had I not been able to say to them, "I know what it's like to be in an abusive relationship. I know how scary it is to have to get out of that situation."

> "I can see how all that I experienced has equipped me with the ability to recognise people's trauma and have compassion and understanding ..."

That's just one side of it, but gosh, Jane, there is so, so much. But that energy, yes, it's always been there. In 1992, I came across a book by Louise L. Hay called *You Can Heal Your Life.* I soaked up every single word. That was my first major turning point in life because I then lived by that book. It was my Bible. And within two years of having picked that book up, I got out of that abusive relationship, that marriage. I walked away with the clothes on my back and my child, and I started a brand new business. Everything took off almost immediately.

Within three months of walking away from that marriage, I had a new apartment, which I fully furnished and I had a brand new car. When I walked away, I had nothing, okay? This is just how powerful spirit is, or the power of your own conviction when you do something and you know that it's the right thing for you. Everything around you conspires to support you and it all just happens. The magic happens.

Then the major shifts came. The breakup from my ex-husband was extremely traumatic because the harassment still continued. I said to my good friend (I'm laughing now), "I think I'm going to have him *bumped off.* I'm going to hire a hit man." *[Laughing]*

She said to me, "For *goodness sake*, Michelle, before you do anything stupid like that, just go and see this woman. She can help you cut the karma." And it was those words, 'cut the karma', where I thought, *Oh, okay. That sounds like a slightly better option than hiring a hit man!* *[Laughing and giggling]*

Without a jail sentence. *[Laughing]*

Yes indeed. So I went off to this lady for healing and I started working on myself. Within eighteen months, my spiritual guide Kuthumi went, "Ta dah, I'm here." The rest, as they say, is history.

For those unfamiliar with your work, Michelle, what actually happened?

Well, I had to run a meditation group one morning. The lady who usually conducted the meditations had to go away on an emergency family call. I was a bit nervous, but I knew most of the girls, so I began taking them through a little visualisation.

That opened the doors for Kuthumi to start talking through me, and that's exactly what happened. The next thing I remember was opening my eyes and looking around and everyone had eyes as huge as saucers and jaws hanging open. I didn't have a clue what had happened, so they all told me. It was quite amazing, but I didn't feel comfortable with being completely unconscious, so I made a deal with him: "Okay, I will be a vessel through which you can deliver the information, but there needs to be a level of me participating consciously in what's going on."

That's how the channelling occurred from there. It was, for me, like falling asleep and beginning to dream, and you're in the dream and experiencing the dream, but your body is in bed. So, when spirits are speaking through me, it's like hearing a narration and observing the movie that's playing out. When I've finished channelling, it's like waking up from a dream. There are bits and pieces I can remember very clearly and other pieces just on the tip of my tongue or just on the edge of consciousness. But if there is something that is important that I need to remember, I am able to go to the data bank and extract that information and remember it. Don't ask me how that happens. I don't know.

Can I ask you who Kuthumi is? How you would explain him?

He's an Ascended Master – someone who has incarnated into human form, mastered the lessons and completed his journey. Now he's guiding, teaching and supporting humanity from a different realm – a realm we cannot see but most certainly a realm which exists. As human beings, we identify with things by a name, so he uses Kuthumi, one of his many incarnations.

Other incarnations he has had are supposed to be Moses; the Shah Jahan Mahal, who built the Taj Mahal; Pythagoras; St Francis of Assisi; Balthazar, one of the three wise men; and then most recently as Kuthumi, who appeared to Helena Blavatsky, the founder of the Theosophical Society. El Morya and St Germain interacted with her quite regularly too. She called these messengers who would materialise and write letters to her 'The Mahatmas'.

Kuthumi can be traced back to Kashmir in India in the mid-1800s. He's had many lives, and he's had to deal with everything we face, which is why he's in a position to be able to guide people, like many of the other Ascended Masters do too.

I started channelling Kuthumi in 1996 and Archangel Michael would pop through occasionally. Then Mary Magdalene in 2006 or 2007 and then Guinevierre.[2]

Initially, I facilitated guided meditations for big groups. Then people started asking me for personal one-on-one sessions. By 1998, I had started putting little workshops together, and from there it grew. So, I was doing regular support groups and writing courses. The *99 Star Code Tablets* came through in 1999 and I ran workshops round them.

From 1996 until now, I have also studied numerology and the properties of crystals. I used to do crystal healing, but eventually I had to hone my skills into the channelling because it was

---

2   Guinevierre is the spelling given to Michelle for Guinevere in her channellings.

taking up so much of my time. It became the primary focus of my work. Then I also did writing of the courses in between and travelling and teaching.

The work has continued to evolve until I now take the information that's being channelled and integrate it into a workshop that can be applied and lived by. It's important that the information be understood, integrated and also digested in a practical, tangible way. I was channelling an immense amount of information and I found people had become channelling junkies and wanted more and more, but nothing was being integrated.

That's when the big change and the turning point came for me, at the end of last year. Through all sorts of circumstances, I had to make many changes. It was very intense, which was why I called it the 'Pathway of the Extreme Lightworkers'. If you want an adrenalin rush of a spiritual nature, well then, this is the kind of thing you can do.

But you need to be at a point in your life where you *really* want to see change. You can't just scan through teachings and go, "I don't feel like looking at that today. Maybe in a month's time." It's like a domino effect: when one thing changes, everything seems to change. That can lead to some very intense shifts in one's life, which at times are overwhelming. It feels like everything is crashing around you, but in actual fact it's just the false structures falling down and making way for all the new to come through, which generally you only tend to see in hindsight, not when you're in the midst of the chaos. That's life.

> "It's like a domino effect: when one thing changes, everything seems to change."

I've also learned medieval astrology, which has been an amazing additional tool because I'm taking all the information I've channelled up until this point and now understanding it on a much deeper level; I'm seeing it from a different perspective.

Yes, well you and I are both 'converts' to medieval astrology. What would you say to anybody who says, "Oh, it's just a load of rubbish."?

Of course the first thing I say to them is, "Give me your date, place and time of birth and let me have a look at a few things." That tends to shut them up pretty quickly. *[Laughing]* But seriously, when people ask, "How on earth can we be governed by planets that are out there in the sky?" the first thing I say is that the moon is a planet and the moon affects everything on earth: the oceans, the tides, the growing phases, the conception, gestation and birth phases of animals. It's kind of like, without the moon, we don't exist. We can look at the sun too.

For Christians, I will point out that the Bible does speak about the messages written in the heavens and how astrology and astronomy were utilised in many different ways at many different times in history. All their farming and harvesting was conducted in alignment with different phases of the moon and the different sun cycles. There are so many references to this kind of thing in the traditional, ancient, medieval and astrological systems that go back to, I think, 100BC. Everything then was basically done following astrology aspects. The astrologists were right hands to the kings and queens *and* to the popes. It got lost during the sixteenth and seventeenth centuries and it is returning. But if people just sit and think about, as I say, the moon and the sun and how that affects us, and then apply a little bit of logic to it, it tends to make a lot more sense eventually.

Can you tell me more about this medieval astrology and what you mean by 'your blueprint' and what insight it gave you into your life?

Over the years I've been channelling, this blueprint was often mentioned, and I understood it to be a map of our life. However, when I got involved in medieval astrology (which is also called Ancient Christian astrology) and I looked at the wheel of the natal horoscope, it hit me like a ton of bricks … because there I saw the blueprint. It's this wheel of life with the twelve segments, twelve aspects of your life path that each contribute to your collective journey. These twelve aspects relate to the planets as they appear at the moment you take your first breath. That snapshot of time reveals the relationships between the planets, the aspect of each planet that affects your own life's journey, and whether it is a challenging aspect or an easier aspect, where it enhances your gifts and your talents.

Studying this helped me see how the nature of spirit animates us through the universal significators and the universal archetypes, which are embodied in what we understand these different planets to mean.[3] Their language combines to create a symphony which communicates itself through us. If we don't know what we're dealing with, what the chords or notes are, it becomes more like a screeching of violence and a completely distorted sound, and that's how I felt at times on the inside. You know something needs to change and you know you need to do something different, but you don't know where to start. It's not a magnificent symphony that makes your hair stand on end and makes you just want to cuddle up in a ball and listen to it.

Utilising people's blueprints, I'm now able to help them apply the information in relation to what that particular blueprint holds for them. So, it takes them further along the map and deeper into their personal world.

Understanding this blueprint helped me to see what my fears were, why they were there, where they stem from. So I could begin to make peace with certain things that I had experienced. I stopped taking things personally. It wasn't about me being bad. It wasn't because I wasn't good enough or I had the wrong dress on. It wasn't my body's fault because my body had begun to change. And one of the ways I had rebelled against the attention that my body attracted – which *I believed* my body attracted and led to the sexual abuse – was to gain weight.

> "I understand now why those things happened, what fate means and what it means to rise above your fate."

I gained a huge amount of weight over a period of nine years. But working with astrology and beginning to make peace with all of that, I was able to lose all the weight. I had piled on forty-odd kilos and I've lost it all. It took time to get there, but I could then understand my children better, why I react to certain things in certain ways and how, at specific times in my life, there were things playing out because that was the theme. It brought clarity. It brought understanding, and with that clarity and understanding I could let it go and move forward. So, that's how understanding that blueprint made such a big difference to me.

When I discovered medieval astrology, it revealed to me so many other levels of myself, and so I was able to come to terms with a lot of what had happened because I could then see that was part

---

3   In astrology, specifically, a significator is a planet ruling a house and a universal archetype is a universal principle or force that affects the human psyche and human behaviour on many levels.

of my blueprint. I understand now why those things happened, what fate means and what it means to rise above your fate. Implementing what needed to be done in order to rise above those patterns was excruciatingly painful but, oh, it was so liberating.

I have to say, there have been so many little moments in time that have contributed to the major changes in my life. Yes, I have repeated what some people would interpret as 'mistakes' … but I like to say, "You know what? I had a lot to do in this lifetime, so I just did it all!" *[Laughing]* So tick that one off – first husband. Then second husband. Third … Okay, so that's all done and dusted! What's next? Four children? Okay. That's done, too. *[Laughing]*

Bless you, Michelle. You could be called a glutton for punishment, but as you say, what brilliant empathy it gives you and compassion for others. That's the gift, isn't it?

Absolutely. When I turned forty, it was a huge turning point for me. I've just turned forty-five, so from the age of forty up until now, I've had the most enlightening journey of all because of everything I've experienced and all the support and guidance I've had from Kuthumi-Agrippa and Mary Magdalene.[4] It was a whole other level of consciousness inside of me which woke up.

I'm sure it's how these guys feel when they start at the bottom of Mount Kilimanjaro and the exhilaration when they plant the flag at the top of that mountain. It's the only thing I can associate it with.

So, how do you personally use the medieval astrology, Michelle, in order to help you navigate your life's path?

Well, I look at what the focus is for each year and each month. So, for instance, I know for this particular year from the fourth of January 2012, to the fourth of January 2013, my primary focus is around my career. This is a point in my life where destiny is taking over. And as each month goes by, by following my chart I know what I need to concentrate on. It's an awesome tool to have. Knowing what I need to concentrate on has made it so much easier for me to respond to opportunities.

The other way I've used astrology is to ensure I don't travel under a Mercury Retrograde.[5] That's very important because that's when people's luggage goes missing, flights are delayed, transport has hiccups, we're more prone to travel accidents, people get lost and they just don't arrive; it's cancellations at the last minute.

That's how it was with my one trip to Ireland. Actually, my goodness, Jane, I think it was that trip when I saw you.

It was. I'm so relieved you said that because I knew there was something out of synch. I loved your channelling at Woodhenge, but everything else felt incomplete and unsatisfactory somehow.

When I started learning about what the Mercury Retrograde was all about, I thought, *My God, that sounds like my trip overseas in October 2007.* And I looked back and Mercury was in retrograde.

---

4   Kuthumi's name changed to Kuthumi-Agrippa as he himself went to a higher level of consciousness.

5   Three or four times a year, Mercury passes the earth in its orbit. This creates the illusion that Mercury is spinning backward. As Mercury rules communication, travel, and technology, all of these areas go haywire for about three weeks.

I was like *That's it. I've learnt that lesson. I'm not going anywhere under a Mercury Retrograde.* I won't ever forget that trip. That's why I remember you so distinctly. That trip sticks in my mind because it was so challenging.

Even my oldest son – he's in London – I'll get a text message from him saying, "Mum, is Mercury in retrograde? Everything is going wrong."

It's a lesson we have all learned. Watch out for Mercury Retrograde!

I see you've renamed your trips, Soul Odyssey, Michelle. I'm so pleased because they're definitely pilgrimages, not just trips. They are so rich.

You're absolutely right. It is a pilgrimage. I've been thinking about changing the wording, so you've just given me the confirmation I need to go ahead and do that.

Excellent. You are, to me, the epitome of a modern Pilgrim Mother, Michelle. You go to these far-flung places in trust that everything's unfolding perfectly.

Thank you. Along the road of my journey with Kuthumi-Agrippa and Mary Magdalene, I was guided to take people to these sacred sites around the world, so specific energy activations could be done there to support Mother Earth. All who travelled with me also experienced huge transformation and change.

I can't say exactly what happened or how people's lives were changed to that degree. I put it down to that almighty presence of spirit at these sacred sites. As you so rightly say, they were 'pilgrimages.' So the pilgrim undergoes that whole transformation.

How on earth did you manage all these pilgrimages with the four children, Michelle? The demands of being a mother alongside your calling?

That has been very difficult, Jane, to be honest with you. The first few times, I tried to deal with it by taking my three youngest children with me. There's a fifteen-year gap between my oldest son and my eleven-year-old. My oldest son, Dean, was quite independent at that stage, but taking my three youngest wasn't the solution. Unfortunately, I couldn't concentrate fully on what needed to be done because they were still little ones and needed my attention.

However, it wasn't long before I decided to end my second marriage. That was a blessing in disguise because when I travelled, I left my three youngest with their father. I can't even describe to you the heartache I would feel leaving the children behind and how deeply I missed them and really pined after them. I just had to say, "Suck up, put on your big girl panties now; you've got a job to do. Before you know it, the two weeks will be gone and you'll back home and you will have your babies back." It was a matter of just having to deal with that longing, and it was hard.

> "I can't even describe to you the heartache I would feel leaving the children behind ..."

I can imagine. Is there one place of pilgrimage that stands out in your mind?

It's difficult to say one particular place. Egypt is definitely very special to me. I've travelled there six times, and after every single one of the journeys – the pilgrimages – something big in my life changed. So, I do have a very strong affinity with Egypt, and the White Desert was absolutely incredible. But then there are others: standing in Petra and in Israel at the Wailing Wall; being in Glastonbury, where I just didn't want to leave; and Tintagel also was such a beautiful place. I could have just sat on top of the hills there with the seagulls twittering in my ears and I would have disappeared into another world. It wouldn't have mattered. And when I walk the streets of London, I'm, "Oh my goodness, I know this place." The architecture in London, when I see it, there's another level of remembrance there. Halong Bay in Vietnam too. In fact, there's a unique and special energy in all of the places I've been to.

And now at this point, it seems to me you've come through massive changes – in your work and personal life – and it's all come good.

Yes, it has. I also believe it was as a result of taking time out to be with myself. I was on my own for about three and half years. During that time, I made the conscious choice to really get to the bottom of who I am and the nature of my relationships. I wanted to understand my personal complexities and the wounds I was carrying, which seemed to be perpetuating different patterns emerging in my relationships. The same patterns were there; they just had different faces.

The transformation that happened as a result meant I could recognise what I really wanted in a relationship. It boils down to a few simple things: that we can bring out the best in each other; we can grow together; respect each other; and have mutual, unconditional love.

I didn't know at the time that the man I was destined to be with was under my nose and I was seeing him every single day. So, in actual fact I was discussing what I was going through with him and we became very close friends. It was amazing. I didn't think he would be completely open to what I do, and it was just so beautiful the way everything unfolded and the tapestry came together. I've experienced support and unconditional love like never before by allowing myself to let it in. I realised my defences were so strong, because of my past experiences, that I wouldn't let anything come close enough to penetrate those walls. I would lash out and hurt before being hurt and I would leave before being left. So yes, there were many things that I needed to do and learn so much from. It's a good place that I find myself in now.

Wonderful. It's lovely to see that you have got that sort of relationship because there are an awful lot of people on their spiritual path who seem to be on their own, perhaps thinking that a man would be a distraction from their spiritual path. I also wonder whether there's something deep within 'pushing' for singlehood that has to be shifted, for example, if they have lived previous lives in convents. But it's great that you're showing a new way. Things seem to have shifted for you. I'm interested in what shifts you see happening in 2012 which people are talking about as a time of huge change.

For me personally, I see it as the shift in the collective consciousness where this is a major turning point in terms of how people relate to the world, and themselves. People are waking up to the fact that there's an essence in their lives, which has been lacking.

2012 is about people reaching a point of no return – their personal break points where they say, "I can't continue like this anymore." And I'm seeing it with the people that I'm dealing with.

But that is where the courage and the determination are now gaining momentum as more and more people want to experience something different.

I don't believe it's about huge doom and gloom. I think it's more of a spiritual revolution rather than the world coming to an end. It's perhaps the old ways of the world ending and a new way being initiated.

Thank you for that. I've heard you say, "The teacher has to master the lesson before it can be taught." There's a lot in your work about leading by example. From your own experience, what would you wish to pass on to others, wherever they are on their path?

The most important thing for me, Jane, was deciding I needed to do something different if I was to move past pain and suffering. Only I could do that. I wanted to find the way to make those changes happen. Personally, I was led to astrology, which became my means of delving deeper into myself. Regardless of what tool is used, the most important thing to know is yourself.

"... send the prayer out into the heavens and trust that the answer will and does come."

Once you've gained that level of clarity, you're then in a position to make informed choices and take action to experience a different outcome. That for me has been the most life-changing and has empowered me to lead by example, especially when it comes to encouraging people to persevere with any change they really deeply want in their lives. Persevere and make the commitment to yourself and don't give up on that.

There is always a way out, and where there's a will, there's a way. That's where that saying comes from. And ask for the help; send the prayer out into the heavens and trust that the answer will and does come. The trick is to get out of your own way. Feel the fear but do it anyway.

Thank you so much, Michelle, for sharing your amazing experiences.

Thank *you* so much. I really appreciate the opportunity to tell my story.

I cannot even begin to imagine some of the hardships Michelle has had to endure. When you look at someone else's life from the outside, they can appear to 'have it made'. I looked at Michelle and thought she was some sort of Superwoman – following her spiritual path, revered channeller at the pinnacle of her craft, leading pilgrimages round the world, and all of this with four children. I was in awe. Her life seemed to be effortless, everything just falling into place, as if graced by Mary Poppins.

It wasn't until January 2012 when I read an article she had written on her Facebook page about her struggles that I saw another side to her. I was aghast. I would never have guessed. I likened the image to a swan gliding across the water with ease, while there's plenty of effort and activity going on beneath the surface. When I heard Michelle's story, I was even *more* impressed by her. I definitely had to share it.

It's so easy to look at other people's seemingly charmed lives from the outside and think, *It's all right for you! What do you know about struggle?* But most of us have no idea what's going on beneath the surface or what's happened to bring them to that place of apparent ease and success.

I identified so much with the heartache Michelle felt on leaving behind her children when she set off on her foreign pilgrimages. Leaving my children, however temporarily, was one of the hardest things I had to do during my corporate career. I transitioned from public sector teaching to my corporate career on 7 October 1987. How do I remember it so precisely? Because it was my younger daughter's seventh birthday — and that day I started my training as a financial adviser in London. To hide my dismay I spent the train journey pretending to be lost in my book. Even now I can remember its title — *The Secret Self: A Century of Short Stories by Women*.[b] Secret indeed! When I arrived at the training venue, a smiling fellow trainee greeted me with, "We've just travelled opposite each other on the train! I nearly said something, but you seemed immersed in your book." Believe me, I don't usually manage a whole train journey without speaking even a few words to a fellow passenger. Maybe the Universe had sent me a friendly companion to take my mind off the separation, but I was oblivious. At least I had his company on my way home.

I reflect on the stark contrast between Michelle's early life and her twins'. For me Michelle is living proof that patterns can definitely be broken. There is no need to be victims of our circumstances and use that as a constant excuse for not sorting out our lives. We can each choose how we respond to our situations, however harsh. Michelle has shown that you can use the times of darkness to fuel the times of light. It can teach great compassion and a deeper empathy towards those who cross your path. When you move out of the darkness, you become a beacon, a way-shower to encourage each navigator. May we all ignite the flame in our lives and shine our light in the world.

"… patterns can be broken. There is no need to be victims of our circumstances and use that as a constant excuse for not sorting out our lives. We can each choose how we respond to our situations…"

JANE NOBLE KNIGHT

Final Words
by Jane Noble Knight

The Pilgrim Mother

Wow! What a rich collection of heart-to-heart conversations I have had. How blessed am I to have spent time with these fabulous women. How nourished am I by their stories.

As I reflect back on these exchanges, my abiding feeling is one of deep inner peace. However different their lifestyle, each woman has found her own inner sanctum, her reason for being and her True Self.

Amanda Reed sold her home, all her possessions and cashed in her savings policies at the age of fifty-one to successfully follow her acting dream, which she had almost forgotten until a friend reminded her; Sue Allan, single mother of four sons, published her first book at fifty and is now a much sought after pilgrimage leader and expert on the Pilgrim families and Gainsborough Old Hall; Julie Dunstan overcame cancer while continuing to help others, on a paid and voluntary basis, and safeguard the future of historically significant Scrooby Manor; Katherine Woodward Thomas spent many years struggling with addictions, then founded the non-profit 'In Harmony with the Homeless' project, before becoming the bestselling author of 'Calling In 'The One', creating the 'Conscious Uncoupling' programme and co-creating 'Feminine Power'; Shelley Bridgman made the ultimate change – that of her gender – to become an award-winning stand-up comic, key note speaker and psychotherapist whilst retaining the support of her family; Marie Laywine left her daughters with their father, at much personal cost, to pursue an independent life as an artist and free her daughters from her 'Mother's Agenda' whilst still playing a supportive role in their lives; Nirjala Tamrakar Wright triumphed over cultural and financial challenges to become Nepal's first professional female mountain biker and also the *only* Nepalese mountain biker to compete in the World Cup; Suki Kaur-Cosier left her three sons with their father and grandparents, without becoming estranged from them, and now fuses her passions for culture, diversity and food into her company, Cooking Matters; and Michelle Manders survived her own horrendous childhood to become a loving mother of four providing spiritual support to many and leading pilgrimages all over the world.

I compare these women with what we know of the Pilgrim Mothers who set sail in the *Mayflower* with their families or employers. These modern Pilgrim Mothers are also co-creating a New World; they have a cause that is bigger than themselves as an individual; they are on a mission that they cannot *not* pursue; they keep on going … through the darkest of times; they show courage in the face of adversity; they seek independence; they are mindful of their families; they support and add value to their communities; and they are leaving lasting legacies.

Some of their journeys have taken them to different countries – and in some cases different continents. They learned from their experiences. What they discovered was that the greatest journey is the one within – to their deepest Self. It reminds me of this lovely quote my friend, Jane Williams, sent me but whose source I have been unable to locate – Pilgrim: journeys to foreign lands and finds home in the heart. That to me sums up the experience of inner peace – the feeling of coming home. We travel through life's varied landscapes and experiences – our 'foreign lands' – and find our way home. It's within us all the time.

So can everyone find their 'way home'?

I believe so. Yes. Absolutely. If I can do it after my own personal journeys, so can others.

However, I recognise that for anyone who is in a dark place at the moment, it can seem like an impossible vision to hold. If that is you, take heart. Every single one of the women in this book (myself included) has been in those depths. It is often the turning point. I look back at moments of enlightenment when everything seemed so fabulous – love and light, love and light – and then all hell broke loose! Friends I had had for years fell out of my life – often painfully; more recent friendships also fell by the wayside; I got divorced after over thirty years of marriage; I was made redundant and every door that opened for new roles swiftly slammed shut; I moved from a lovely big house in the country where I had lived for 14 years to a jerry-built rented house whose owners served me notice to quit after a year, which led to me being displaced for a while and then spending most of 2011 travelling round in a motorhome with my two dogs; I lost my comfort blanket of large amounts of investments; and I really had no idea where life was leading me. Nevertheless I kept faith that all was as it was meant to be and at some point I would emerge from the fog. I did. And quite honestly I would not have had it any other way. How else could I listen with empathy and a sense of sisterhood *now* to the amazing stories of these courageous women, had I not been on my own adventure? And yes, it *is* an adventure. It *is* a rollercoaster … and at any moment life can change for the better. You see, I believe we are all responsible for our lives. What we focus on, we attract into our life. All right, I admit it. I did at times think, *What on earth am I doing choosing this?* And yet I survived. After all, predictable films where the main character has no challenges are really boring. Whatever else, my life is never dull.

As Katherine Woodward Thomas remarked about her own journey, "We have to go into the very bottom of the human experience in order to bring light there. It's one thing to talk about the light, but it's another thing if you're having an experience of light and you try and describe it to someone who's not, who's in the darkness. And it's another thing again to actually go into the darkness and then find your way out by discovering the light within you, one step at a time, so that you're then able to lead people out of the darkness with you."

And how exactly does this happen?

Well, through speaking with these modern women pioneers and writing *The Inspiring Journeys* series, I have extracted this list of practices to assist you on your journey.

The 12 Steps to Pilgrim Motherhood

1. Get accustomed to STILLNESS.
2. Create a nurturing SPACE for yourself.
3. Trust your inner SIGHT.
4. SHARE who you truly are.
5. Follow your SOUL's calling.
6. Kindle your SPARK of passion.
7. Notice SIGNS and SYNCHRONICITIES.
8. Offer your life in SERVICE.
9. Take one STEP at a time towards your dream.
10. SING the praises of yourself and others.
11. Define SUCCESS on your own terms.
12. Live your most heroic STORY.

In the end it is *your* story – no one else's. Whichever storyline compels you to action, follow where it leads. If you really are struggling to imagine a future other than continuing on your current path and that isn't particularly appealing, think back to your childhood. What did you *love* doing then? Often the clues are there but we can lose sight of them along the way or be discouraged from that direction. It's never too late to go back and rekindle that childhood passion. You choose the life *you* want to lead, not the one *others* want you to lead. They have their own. It's selfish to expect to have a say in yours too.

As the Peace Pilgrim said, "A pilgrim is a wanderer with purpose." Make sure it's *your* purpose and you enjoy the wanderings. Take your time. Remember, there is always help along the way. You just have to look up and watch out for it and don't forget to ask for assistance when you need it. Pilgrims can travel with families and communities, you know. We don't have to do it on our own. There are guides, staging posts, pit stops, service stations, oases, hostelries, inner SatNavs, compasses, maps, uncharted territories beyond the edges of the maps … I could go on. Whatever route you choose, if you have never travelled that way before, you are a pioneer on your pathway to inner peace, your journey home. You are blazing your trail. Ploughing your furrow. Enjoying your ride.

In the wise words of Ursula K LeGuin, "It is good to have an end to journey towards; but it is the journey that matters, in the end."

"When you move out of the darkness, you become a beacon, a way-shower to encourage each navigator.
May we all ignite the flame in our lives and shine our light in the world."

JANE NOBLE KNIGHT

Acknowledgements

To my fabulous daughters, Siân and Rebecca, for all your support, and to Jo, my 'adopted' daughter.

To my sister, Wendy, and brother-in-law, Ian Connor, and their four-legged Lhasa Apso 'bruiser', Domino.

To my own four-legged doggy companions, Bran and Holly, and a special mention to all my animal companions over the years. Never forgotten.

To my wonderful support team … Wendy Millgate of Wendy & Words; Eleanor Piredda for marketing support; Siân-Elin Flint-Freel for helping with my first book launch; Shari Thompson of Green Jelly Marketing for social media; Julia Power for transcriptions; Isabel Gainford for the original book cover branding ideas; Stephanie J Hale, Peggy McColl and Julia McCutchen for information on writing, publishing and launching books; Tanya Back for book cover design and typesetting; Nirjala Tamrakar Wright for your beautiful cover image; Sara Moseley for my photos; Katharine Dever for midwifing The Pilgrim Mother; and Anita Noyes-Smith of Virgin Astrology who continues to astound me with the value of her guidance on my life's path.

To my very first Pilgrim Mother Mentoring Group, some of whom have already been mentioned in other roles: Anna Goodwin, Eleanor Piredda, Esther Morson-Mills, Rosy Banger, Shari Thompson, Shirley Harvey, Siân-Elin Flint-Freel, Sue Wilkinson and Suryah Magda Ray. Together we are pioneering new ways of working.

To my Feminine Power friends: Nyali Muir, Anne Risaria Langley, Barbara Junceau, Nancy Frankel, Catharina Van Leeuwen and Vicky Van Praag.

To the women's networking groups to which I belong: my local Women in Rural Enterprise (WiRE) groups in Newport, Shropshire run by Maggie Hollinshead and Penny Eccleston and in Cannock, Staffordshire run by Anna Goodwin and Mary Freeman; and Forward Ladies run locally by Sue France.

To the Pilgrim Mother Entrepreneurs in my first book: Carry Somers, Dawn Gibbins, Gill Fielding, Gina Lazenby, Katharine Dever, Marie-Claire Carlyle, Penny Power, Rachel Elnaugh and Stephanie J Hale. A special thanks to Dawn for the fabulous launch of my first book at her home in Cheshire … and to Carry, Gill, Marie-Claire and Rachel who joined my friends, old and new, to make it such a special occasion, always to be remembered. Thank you all for making it such a special occasion. And to Gina, who was in Australia when I launched and offered her home for a London gathering to celebrate my first book and the legacy of Pilgrim Mothers. That was another special evening.

To the new women friends I am making through my work and whose stories will be gracing future books in the series.

To the amazing *Mayflower* Pilgrim Mothers whose story inspired me and changed my life forever.

And of course to all the fabulous Pilgrim Mothers in this book. I am honoured that you shared your stories with me so that I might in turn share them with a wider audience. Thank you.

I love you all.

About the Author

As long as she can remember Jane has been fascinated by people. Unsurprisingly, she studied sociology and psychology at Liverpool University. Jane's forty years' experience spans social work, sales, teaching, training and coaching, the last thirty of which have been in people development. In 1999 Jane became a freelance training consultant, heading up national training teams with many well-known organisations, mainly in financial services. A project in which she played a leading role was runner-up in a Financial Times Arts and Business Award.

Alongside her corporate work Jane studied metaphysics and qualified in complementary therapies such as Hypnotherapy, Past Life Regression and Colour Mirrors. Jane is a lifelong learner. No 'learning junkie' who studies for study's sake, once Jane finds something of value, she applies it – she walks her talk.

In 2009 Jane took part in a BBC1 House Swap programme. A presenter's question led her to discover the story of the Pilgrim Mothers and subsequently take up the quest to learn more about them and the hidden stories of other pioneering women. Along the way she bought a motorhome and set off with her two dogs to wherever she was drawn, meeting amazing women and recording their stories.

This second book is a result of Jane's continuing journey. It is a reflection of this 'calming, kind but dynamic' woman's passion for empowering others by unearthing and sharing the gems of wisdom she has this uncanny ability to find wherever Life leads her.

You are warmly invited to find out more about Jane's adventures and how to get involved at www.thepilgrimmother.com or by emailing jane@thepilgrimmother.com.

End Notes

a   Jane Noble Knight, *The Inspiring Journeys of Women Entrepreneurs: Exploring New Ways of Business That Answer Your Calling*, Noble Knight Publishing, 12 February 2013.

b   Hermione Lee (Editor), *The Secret Self: Short Stories by Women*, Dent, 1985.

Lightning Source UK Ltd.
Milton Keynes UK
UKOW01f1935290713

214580UK00010B/1145/P